BODY GUARDS

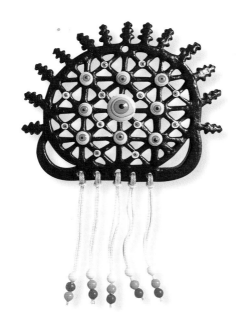

BODY GUARDS

PROTECTIVE AMULETS & CHARMS

Desmond Morris

ELEMENT

Shaftesbury, Dorset • Boston, Massachusetts • Melbourne, Victoria

First published in Great Britain in 1999 by
ELEMENT BOOKS LIMITED
Shaftesbury, Dorset, SP7 8BP

Published in the USA in 1999 by
ELEMENT BOOKS INC
160 North Washington Street, Boston, MA 02114

Published in Australia in 1999 by
ELEMENT BOOKS
and distributed by Penguin Australia Ltd
487 Maroondah Highway, Ringwood, Victoria 3134

Designed by
THE BRIDGEWATER BOOK COMPANY LIMITED

ELEMENT BOOKS LIMITED
Editorial Director Sue Hook
Project Manager Shirley Patton
Editor Alison Wormleighton

THE BRIDGEWATER BOOK COMPANY
Art Director Terry Jeavons
Designer Michael Whitehead
Editorial Director Fiona Biggs
Managing Editor Anne Townley
Project Editor Caroline Earle
Picture Research Vanessa Fletcher
Photography Guy Ryecart and Trish Gant

Printed and bound in Great Britain by Butler & Tanner Ltd

British Library Cataloguing in Publication
data available

Library of Congress Cataloging in Publication
data available

ISBN 1–86204–572–0

CONTENTS

AUTHOR'S FOREWORD

IN MY TRAVELS around the world studying the human species I noticed that almost everywhere I went people had some kind of lucky charm. The form it took varied from country to country and culture to culture. In each place the favourite local charm was treated very seriously and endowed with helpful, magical properties. Sometimes it was meant to protect its owners from bad luck, sometimes to bring them good luck. Always there was a fascinating history or symbolic background to the charms. I began to make a personal collection of them, trying to understand what made each of them so special.

My many journeys, recording human behaviour and making television films, took me to more than 70 countries, and over the years my collection of charms and amulets grew and grew until I had several hundred examples. Filming in remote parts of Africa, I found that the local women often

The sacred turtle from China worn as an amulet to bring wisdom and a long life.

carried fertility figures in their clothing to increase their chances of becoming pregnant. (How different from the West, where young women often carry contraceptives to increase their chances of not becoming pregnant.) In the Middle East I encountered endless examples of religious amulets, from sacred hands to inscribed passages from the Koran. Studying gestures in southern Italy, I found that the centuries-old tradition of protecting yourself from the Evil Eye was still thriving and was supported by a whole variety of special actions and charms. In Scandinavia I found that many of the old Viking legends live on in the form of modern amulets. In California I discovered a whole new wave of charms emerging in the form of magic crystals and gems. This New Age fascination with crystal healing and protection has spread rapidly and is now found all across the Americas and much of Europe.

Most of the charms and amulets I collected were small objects that were worn or carried on the

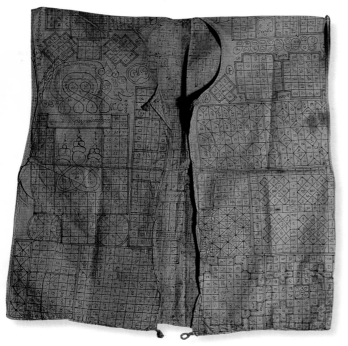

An amuletic shirt from Burma, with magic spells to protect the wearer during journeys or warfare.

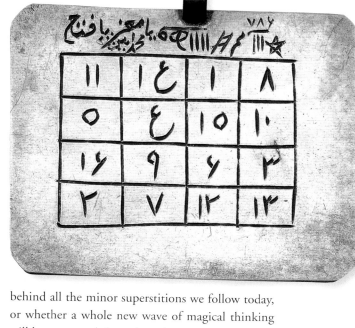

An amulet from Afghanistan, inscribed with a magic square.

body. Some, however, were slightly larger and were intended to protect their owners by guarding their horses, cars, boats or houses. Many drivers will not leave home without their lucky mascot hanging inside their vehicle to keep them safe from accidents. In the Mediterranean some boatmen will not put to sea without a pair of eyes fixed to their boats to outstare the Evil Eye and protect them from drowning. In England, even today, many owners of working horses adorn them with special horse-brasses that will guard the animals against the forces of evil, as they have done for centuries. And countless country cottages, stables and barns still have lucky horseshoes displayed conspicuously on walls or above doors.

These are just a few of the ways in which primitive superstitions survive in this modern era of scientific thinking and computerized information. Even people who do not take the idea of protective amulets seriously will usually have some little object that they keep about them 'just for luck'. They scoff at the idea of magical protection, and insist that their lucky charm is really just a joke, but they hang on to it nevertheless. Old traditions die hard.

In writing this book my main interest has been to record an endlessly fascinating human pursuit, as it survives at the end of the 20th century. I cannot help wondering whether, if someone were to read this book 100 years from now, they would be surprised at how primitive we were in our beliefs, or whether they would be saying, yes, we still do all that, even now. It is impossible to predict whether humanity will leave

behind all the minor superstitions we follow today, or whether a whole new wave of magical thinking will have erupted throughout human society. It will probably all depend on how secure or insecure we become as a result of our technical advances in the years ahead. Technology has brought us many benefits that make us feel much more secure, but until it has removed our fears of such fundamental threats as disease, injury, ageing and death, we will doubtless always feel in need of a little supernatural aid. As long as we suffer from dark, unspoken anxieties and worries, there will probably always be a place in our lives for those curious little objects that I have called…Body Guards.

A protective horse-brass with a central eye to out-stare the Evil Eye. From the Cliffe Castle Museum, Keighly.

THE ARMADILLO FACTOR

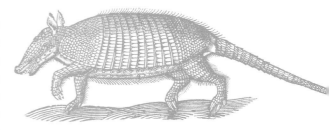

THE ARMADILLO SURVIVES because it is covered in a hard, protective shell. When threatened or attacked, it responds by rolling up into a tight ball. Its tormentor is faced by an impenetrable sphere of thick armour and soon gives up and goes away. After a while, when all is quiet again, the armadillo unrolls itself and wanders away unharmed. Its protective shell is its permanent guardian against the hostile forces of nature.

The human being, by contrast, has a soft, vulnerable body that is all too easily damaged. It gives us great flexibility but it leaves us exposed to many dangers. Occasionally we try to emulate the armadillo and wear some kind of protective shield. Medieval knights went into battle in heavy suits of armour. Modern police forces frequently employ bulletproof vests. Astronauts, deep-sea divers and laboratory technicians wear special suits to guard them from harmful environments. But these are the exceptions. The vast majority of human beings live out their lives in an armourless, shell-free, soft-bodied condition. As a result there is, for many, a craving for some alternative, less cumbersome kind of defence system.

For thousands of years, it has been the custom to employ some sort of protective object that will make its owner feel a little safer when facing the hazards of daily life. These objects have been given a variety of names – amulets, mascots, charms or talismans. Some are worn on the body, others are carried, and still others are placed in their owner's vehicle or building. They work in one of two ways: they either ward off bad luck, or they attract good luck. They are known from almost every culture and from every period in history and even prehistory.

There are three kinds of Body Guard: the personal and particular; the ancient and historical; and the modern and active.

Unlike the armadillo, human beings have no hard shell to protect them.

The personal examples are countless. Many people, especially those in high-risk occupations, possess a private lucky charm. They (often secretly) insist on having it with them whenever they face a personal challenge. Sportsmen and women, actors and actresses, soldiers, sailors and airmen, and others whose regular tasks put them in social or physical danger frequently carry with them some kind of protective object that is special and unique to them.

To give just one extreme example showing how involved and complicated these personal superstitions can become, one famous footballer went through the following extraordinary routine every time he played a game.

The infant Jesus playing with the Virgin Mary's protective rosary.

1 He did not shave on the morning of a match.

2 He always carried a key-ring with a thistle motif.

3 He took with him to the football stadium an old tennis ball.

4 He put in his pocket a miniature football boot he found on the pitch one afternoon.

5 He always wore a small, star-shaped medal.

6 He always used peg 13 for hanging his clothes up in the dressing room.

7 He always put on his old playing top, from his first club, underneath his current one.

8 He always bounced a football three times on the wall of the tunnel as he went on to the pitch.

9 When running out onto the pitch before the game he always kicked a ball into the empty net.

10 During the game he always blew his nose as often as possible. He was quoted as saying: 'I don't think I could play without going through these preparations.' And losing a match never put him off, such is the intensity of personal superstitions.

The ancient and historical examples of Body Guards are also numerous, because in earlier days the superstitious beliefs in magical aids were even more common than they are today. But those early examples that no longer have any significance are of limited interest today. They belong to the pages of academic folklore studies.

It is the third group – the active modern survivals – that are of special interest. Examples of common protective objects used by large numbers of people nearly always have an ancient origin, but they have somehow managed to keep their grip on the human imagination long after most other superstitious practices have been forgotten. It is these persistent, widespread examples that deserve our attention and it is these that the present book attempts to assemble together and examine objectively for the first time.

These wooden idols from Afghanistan are hung around the necks of highly valued cattle to keep them safe from the Evil Eye.

DEFINITIONS

THE WORDS AMULET, mascot, charm and talisman have revealing origins. 'Amulet' comes from the Latin *amuletum*, but some claim that its true origin is to be found in the Arab term *hamala*, meaning 'to carry'. An amulet is defined as 'anything worn about the person as a charm or preventative against evil, mischief, disease or witchcraft'.

'Mascot' comes from the French (Provençal) term *masco*, meaning a witch. This, in turn, came from an old French word, *mascotte*, meaning 'a mask' and referring to the mask worn by a sorcerer. Originally it indicated a person or a thing

The conch shell is said to protect its owner from poverty.

that brought good luck, but it gradually became more limited in meaning, referring mostly to small 'lucky objects'.

'Charm', rather surprisingly, comes from the Latin word *carmen*, meaning a 'song'. It relates back to the uttering of magical chants which led to a condition of 'enchantment'.

'Talisman' comes from the greek *telesma*, meaning 'consecrated object' – an object consecrated by the completion of a religious ritual. A talisman is defined as 'a stone, ring or other object engraved with figures or characters, to which are attributed the occult powers of the planetary influences and celestial configurations under which it was made; usually worn as an amulet to avert evil from or bring fortune to the wearer; also medicinally used to impart healing virtue'. In other words, a talisman is an amulet that carries a magical or sacred inscription. To be a true talisman, it must display some lettering, numbers or text, or an abstract symbol or pattern of some kind.

In modern speech, the distinctions can be summed up as follows. An amulet is a small object that protects its owner from harm. A mascot is an object (or person) that brings good luck to its owner or the group it represents. A charm is a small object that brings good luck. A talisman is a magical object with a message or symbol that both protects from bad luck and brings good luck.

A horned hand gesture painted on a small Maltese boat to protect it from the Evil Eye.

The Irish Shamrock, or three-leaf clover, is one of the most popular of all protective amulets.

One other term that deserves a special mention is the Evil Eye. Although amulets are intended to protect their owners from various kinds of misfortune, this leaves open the question of where these misfortunes come from. They may, of course, be completely random. You suffer from them simply because you are in the wrong place at the wrong time. Or they may be the result of stupid or ignorant actions for which you yourself are directly to blame. But superstitious people find both randomness and personal blame hard to accept. They feel that if something bad suddenly happens to them, it must be the result of a supernatural, hostile force.

This 'dark power' has often been conceived as an Evil Eye that transmits its harm simply by staring at its victims. To survive its attack they must somehow avoid eye-to-eye contact. They can do this by confronting it with something it dislikes or fears or by distracting it in some way. Many amulets are designed with this in mind.

There are three kinds of Evil Eye. First, there is the 'innocent' or involuntary Evil Eye. Particular individuals gain a reputation for possessing an Evil Eye that is not under their control. They mean no harm, but they cannot help causing it. They usually gain their reputation because, after they have paid a visit somewhere, there is a sudden and unexpected tragedy. Having no other explanation, people assume that the visitor must have been the cause of it. Sometimes an individual with a squint or some other minor defect is automatically

An amulet, like this one, inscribed with occult, magical symbols is called a talisman.

assumed to possess the 'Eye'. The second type is the malicious or malevolent Eye, possessed by someone who deliberately sets out to cause harm. And the third is the more nebulous, unseen, disembodied, occult Evil Eye. All three versions are feared in many different cultures, and a large number of the amulets described in this book are specifically designed to combat them.

This ancient Roman bronze hand, covered in symbols, was kept in the house to protect the occupants.

Animal Magic
ZOOLOGICAL BODY GUARDS

Since the earliest times, animal images have been employed as totems and mascots. They have also been used in a number of special ways as protective amulets, and this ancient custom is still alive and widespread today. The animal kingdom offers such a variety of symbolism that there are endless ways in which animal images can be called upon to perform protective duties. Sometimes the whole animal is employed and sometimes just one part of it is used, such as the wishbone, the tooth, the claw, the shell or the horn. There is hardly a country in the world today that does not display at least one kind of zoological amulet.

THE SCARAB

The scarab – the sacred beetle of ancient Egypt – is still popular today as a lucky charm, usually mounted on finger-rings, earrings, pendants or brooches. It therefore has one of the longest pedigrees of any amulet in the world, having been magically active for well over 4,000 years.

THE SYMBOLISM OF the scarab gives it a central role in the world of amuletic protection, for it stands for no less than life itself. The humble dung-beetle that the scarab represents became associated, in the minds of the early Egyptians, with such major themes as creation, generation, virility, wisdom, renewal, resurrection and immortality.

The reason such grand themes became attached to so lowly an animal is that the Egyptians misinterpreted the strange actions of dung-beetles. From these misunderstandings two legends arose.

The first resulted from the beetles' action of laboriously rolling spherical pellets of dung across the earth, which the Egyptians related to the way the sun-god rolled the sun across the sky. Heat and life came from the sun, so they concluded that the beetles were symbols of generation. They wore models of the beetles as amulets to give them the strength of the god of creation.

The second legend arose from the Egyptians' observing the beetles digging deep holes into the earth and depositing the transported balls of dung inside them, and then later seeing young beetles emerge from these holes. The Egyptians assumed that the original beetles had been reborn. Concluding that the original beetles were immortal, the Egyptians endowed them with the symbolic properties of eternal renewal and resurrection.

The reality, of course, was that the female beetles laid their eggs on the buried dung-balls. When these eggs hatched, they used the dung as a food source, then pupated and eventually emerged as new adult beetles. This form of life cycle, misinterpreted as rebirth, appealed strongly to the Egyptians, who were obsessed with the afterlife.

So the lowly dung-beetle was seen as possessing two major attributes – the control of the sun *and* immortality. It is little wonder that it became such an important Body Guard and that literally hundreds of thousands of scarab amulets were manufactured in ancient Egypt. Indeed, it is true to say that hardly any other amuletic motif could match it for popularity.

The smallest scarabs were tiny ones attached to pieces of jewellery, while the largest were huge and were meant to protect whole buildings rather than mere individuals. The biggest scarab known, now in the British Museum, is 1.5m (5ft) long and 90cm (3ft) wide, and weighs 1,000kg (2 tons).

In ancient Egypt the scarab was worn by the living to protect them from death, and worn by the dead to ensure their afterlife. During the process of embalming, the scarab amulet was placed reverently on the chest or inside the cavity of the heart.

The fame of the scarab amulet spread outwards from Egypt. Examples have been found in archaeological excavations in Turkey, Syria, Iran, Iraq, Lebanon, Israel and most of the Mediterranean countries. In modern times they are found over much of the world, sold as lucky charms to people who usually know little of their mythological origins or their once powerful, religious role.

THE FISH

As an amulet, the protective fish has staged a spirited comeback in recent years after centuries of neglect. In many countries in the Western world it is now possible to see stylized fish symbols attached to the rear ends of vehicles, their owners proclaiming to those behind them (in the inevitable traffic jams of modern times) that they are guarded from evil by this ancient sign of Christ.

THE CHRISTIAN FISH amulet has gone through three stages during its long history. In the beginning it was a favoured sign of Jesus Christ, the 'fisher of men'. It embodied a secret message at times when the first Christians were suffering persecution. The Greek name for a fish was *icthys*, the letters of which these early Christians read as standing for *Iesous Christos Theou Hyios Soter*, meaning 'Jesus Christ, Son of God, Saviour'.

For several hundred years the fish remained the covert symbol of Christ, but then, when Christianity at last became an acceptable faith, it lost ground to the more overt symbolism of the cross – an abrasive reminder of the way Christ had been tortured on the hill at Calvary. Even then, despite official approval of Christian worship, the cross faced a degree of opposition. Because it was too closely related to older, pagan beliefs, some early leaders of the Christian Church itself tried to prevent its sacred use. However, despite their misgivings, in the fourth century the cross began to take over as the major Christian symbol. The association between the cross on which Jesus Christ had sacrificed his life and the Saviour's image was too close to ignore.

With the rise of the cross symbol came the fall of the ancient fish symbol. It more or less vanished from use until, in the 20th century, born-again Christians were looking for an alternative symbol that was more personal and less associated with the Church. The fish resurfaced and became one of the best-selling Christian travelling companions of modern times.

There is, however, a sting in the tail of this particular fish. In the same way as the cross symbol, it had an earlier, pagan role. For many centuries before the arrival of Christ it had been a sexual symbol, representing the reproductive organs of the Great Goddess. To some it represented the womb, to others the vulva – either way, it was sacred to the goddess. The reason why many people eat fish on a Friday (although they may not realize it) is because Friday takes its name from a Teutonic goddess of love. (In Italy, fish is also eaten on Friday, where the day is called *Venerdì*, after the Roman form of the goddess – Venus.) So, when today's born-again Christians set off in the family car, with a protective fish symbol cheerfully displayed on its rear, it could be argued that they are inadvertently offering a display of sacred female genitals to the driver who is following them.

In non-Christian countries, this sexual symbolism of the fish has remained active across the centuries, and today fish amulets are still worn or displayed as protection against lack of fertility. From fertility to fecundity, to the renewal of life, the image of the fish has been pressed into service in many cultures.

Further confusion has been added in the last few years, with the introduction of a modified, Darwinian fish symbol. This is identical to the Christian one, except for the fact that the fish has now grown two primitive legs. Symbolizing evolution and the protective supremacy of scientific reason over primitive superstition, this fish symbol is the atheist's response to the born-again followers of the faith.

The Darwin fish symbol, which has grown a pair of legs, offering protection to evolutionists.

THE GUARDIAN SERPENT

To many people, the snake is an enemy to be feared and avoided at all costs. Its venom makes it a villain. And yet, in many regions and at many times in history, the snake has been viewed as a sacred, protective power. Snake amulets were being worn at least 3,000 years ago and are still being worn today. How can we explain this contradiction?

THE ANSWER LIES in the snake's ability to renew itself by shedding its skin. When the ancients saw this, they imagined that serpents were immortal. One day, they would see a snake with a dull, damaged skin and with its eyes glazed over. Then, the next day, as if by magic, they would observe the same snake, smooth and glistening and with its eyes once again clear and penetrating. To them it appeared as if the snake was capable of rejuvenating itself, and they came to the conclusion that it must hold the secret of eternal life.

As a result of this misunderstanding (and also perhaps because they recognized that snakes were valuable killers of rodent pests) the ancients came to love and revere the serpent and seek its protection. It became sacred to the god of medicine and a symbol of longevity and immortality. Rings in the shape of snakes twisted around the finger, or with their tails in their mouths, were worn as special guardians against sickness and all forms of ill-health. Larger, more elaborate gold snakes were worn around the arm as bracelets.

It is still possible today to buy snake-rings or bracelets very similar in design to those worn in ancient Egypt, Greece and Rome. Many trinket shops in the Mediterranean and the Middle East display cheap ones for sale and serious jewellers offer more expensive versions in gold or silver. However, their role is now largely decorative, their earlier protective duties having been forgotten, swept away by the widespread modern hatred of poisonous reptiles.

There are, however, some parts of the world where serpent gods are still active. In Zimbabwe, for instance, visitors who are about to risk their lives white-water rafting down the Zambesi river, are today sometimes offered the protection of Nyami-Nyami, the snake river-god, in the form of a small soapstone amulet to wear around the neck. It is a strange little figure, with its body apparently twisted back on itself and with its tail ending up in its mouth. If this is the correct interpretation, it relates Nyami-Nyami to the 'eternity' ring-snakes of the ancient world.

The legend of Nyami-Nyami is that while a hunter of the Batonka tribe was watching an elephant drinking at the Zambesi river he saw a fishing eagle swoop down and catch a large fish in his talons. The hunter realized that there was food in the river and imitated the eagle, diving into the water in search of fish. Unfortunately, he was instead eaten by a crocodile, but his spirit became the snake river-god, Nyami-Nyami. Following this incident, his tribe converted from hunters to fishermen and Nyami-Nyami protected them from the dangers of the Zambesi.

A Nyami-Nyami amulet, worn smooth by use on the great River Zambesi.

For these white-water risk-takers on the Zambesi, wearing a protective Nyami-Nyami amulet is felt to be essential.

THE RABBIT'S FOOT

It seems odd that the rabbit's foot should be the most popular of all modern-day lucky charms. In the 1960s it was reported that no fewer than ten million of them were sold annually in the United States alone, even though logic suggests that they should provide little protection. A Californian roadside sign sums it up well, with the words: 'On curves ahead remember, sonny, that rabbit's foot didn't save the bunny.'

S O WHY *DOES* THE amputated foot of a dead rabbit hold such powerful appeal for the superstitious? A number of theories have been suggested in explanation.

- ♣ Witches were sometimes thought to take the form of rabbits, and fishermen and sailors accordingly regarded the rabbit as a creature of 'ill-omen', sometimes refusing to allow its name to be spoken before going to sea. To carry the foot of a dead rabbit was therefore a way of saying 'I have slain the witch and here is my proof'.
- ♣ Because of their breeding habits, rabbits represent fecundity and are therefore fertility symbols. As such, they protect a person who carries a token of them, making that person more fertile, creative and prosperous. In some countries a woman who wishes to become pregnant will always carry a rabbit's foot hidden in her clothing.
- ♣ Rabbits are born with their eyes open, and it was thought that their ever-alert gaze would provide them with special powers over the Evil Eye.
- ♣ The fact that rabbits touch the ground with their hind feet in front of their forefeet when they are running made the back foot seem somehow unique and magical.
- ♣ In earlier days, the rabbit's foot was used as a powder-puff when applying make-up, especially in theatrical dressing-rooms. When the more modern forms of powder-puff were introduced, actors were loath to throw away their old and trusted rabbits' feet, which had accompanied them through so many stress-filled moments as they prepared to take the stage. So although they were now obsolete, the old rabbits' feet were kept on in the make-up boxes, 'just for luck'. In this way they became strongly associated with theatrical good luck. Their use then spread to other high-risk occupations – from gambling to poaching and from driving racing cars to flying fighter planes.

The recent decline in popularity of the rabbit's foot lucky charm is good news for the rabbits.

The rabbit's foot lucky charm reached its peak of popularity in the first half of the 20th century, especially during the battlefield slaughters of World Wars I and II. It appears to be losing ground now, at the turn of the century, possibly because of the rise of 'animal rights' and vegetarianism. The practice of carrying any part of a dead animal is increasingly being perceived as unethical. The rabbit's foot will probably be slowly phased out in parallel with the wearing of a fur coat.

For those who, despite the changing climate of opinion, still wish to cling to their rabbit's foot Body Guard, it is important to remember that the most effective ones are cut from the left hind leg of the animal. To be even more specific, this foot should be severed at full moon by a cross-eyed person. And it is important to make sure, when you buy one, that the fur has not been dyed. In America at one time it became the custom to dye the fur pink, so as to make the foot look prettier and slightly less like a slaughterhouse left-over, but this 'improvement' was strongly condemned by the seriously superstitious.

You may also wish to perpetuate the old Welsh custom of brushing the forehead of your newborn baby with a rabbit's foot, as a form of pagan 'baptism'. This is considered to give the infant the promise of a lucky life. After this protective ritual the foot should be placed in the baby's cradle or hung more conspicuously above it.

It is bad luck to lose any protective amulet, but for some reason, this was especially so with the rabbit's foot. To lose one was a serious, sometimes desperate matter, foretelling that the owner would be doomed to some early disaster, or even death. For this reason, rabbits' feet tended to be stubbornly persistent lucky charms which, once adopted, were seldom given up.

TOOTH AND CLAW

In lands where large predators rule the wilds, the local people who must encounter these animals develop a fear and respect for them that leads to the birth of many legends and superstitions. Where tigers, lions, leopards, bears and wolves roam free, their powerful weapons — teeth and claws — are viewed with envy by their human neighbours. These are the animals' natural killing tools making human teeth and nails look puny by comparison.

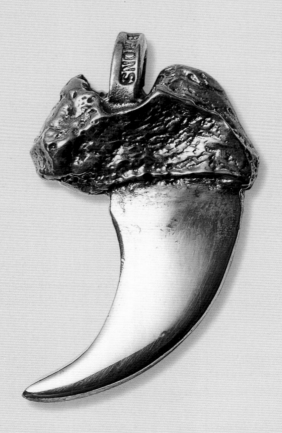

A FTER A PREDATOR has died, its teeth and claws become powerful amulets, jealously guarded by their new, human owners who, in wearing them, hope to gain some of the animal's immense power. Mounted in gold or silver and worn around the neck, a bear's tooth or a tiger's claw carries with it not only the echo of its past power, but also a note of triumph – the great killer is dead, the human being lives!

Tooth amulets and claw amulets appear in the adornments of many cultures. Nearly always, it is believed that they will magically increase the physical strength of the wearer. In some instances there are extra benefits. In certain countries it is said that a bear-claw amulet will also help a woman during childbirth. Elsewhere, a wolf's tooth attached to an infant's body will protect the child from fear and from toothache. In Monte Carlo and other casino cities, a tiger's claw or tooth mounted in gold as an amulet is said to be especially helpful to gamblers. In China the same is true and there the tiger is referred to as 'the gambler's god'.

The sharp claw of an animal makes a valuable amulet because it is thought to embody the power of its previous owner.

This bear's tooth was a valued amulet, serving to protect an Inuit hunter from misfortune.

An Etruscan amulet in the form of a tusk, carved out of basalt and mounted in gold.

A special kind of tooth – a tusk – was sometimes used as a general protective amulet and also as an 'amplifier' of other amulets. Hanging a small tusk from an already powerful charm was believed to increase its strength still further. By definition, tusks are large teeth that protrude from the mouths of animals, such as elephants, walruses, warthogs, various wild pigs and certain deer. Tusks suitable for ameletic use cannot, of course, be large, which rules out all but the smallest of walrus or elephant tusks. In practice, those most commonly employed as amulets are taken from members of the pig family.

Among the Saami or Lapp people of northern Scandinavia the brown bear was viewed as a sacred animal and treated with honour and respect. On occasions when it was hunted, its flesh was only eaten at special ceremonial gatherings and its skeleton was ritually buried in a lifelike posture. This was done so that the slain bear could magically come to life again. The wearing of a bear's-claw amulet was a way of invoking the strength and courage of the great animal, in the hope that these qualities would be transferred to the owner of the pendant.

THE LUCKY ELEPHANT

The Hindu god Ganesha was the elephant-headed son of Shiva and Parvati. The most popular explanation of how the child acquired an elephant's head is that he was decapitated by his angry father. Guarding his mother's privacy while she was taking a bath, he barred even his father from entering the house. Shiva cut off his head, but then regretted his action and offered to replace it with the first one available – that of an elephant.

GANESHA WAS essentially a good-luck god, promising success, prosperity and peace. In particular, he was a 'remover of obstacles' – by the simple means of flattening them with his trunk. It is not surprising that for Hindus he became a popular household guardian.

As a result of Ganesha's reputation for offering help, the elephant itself, in its natural animal form, became known as a symbol of good fortune. The transformation from Indian protective elephant-headed god to Westernized lucky-elephant charm gained momentum in the early part of the 20th century.

These charms grew in popularity, reaching their peak in the 1920s and 1930s when they became part of nearly every charm bracelet in Europe and North America. The small figurines were made out of silver, jade, ivory, onyx, ebony and a variety of other materials. The posture of the elephant was important. To bring good luck to the wearer it had to be shown standing, in a walking pose, and with its trunk raised high and curled back so that it touched the animal's forehead. No other posture carried the good-luck magic.

It has been suggested that the raised-trunk posture was required for the same reason that lucky horseshoes must point upwards – to stop the luck from running out. By curling upwards, the trunk prevents the luck from flowing down and away.

In addition to an amulet to be worn on the body, the elephant also appeared as a guardian of the home. Small black-and-white figurines carved out of ebony, with contrasting tusks of ivory, were placed in the house to keep it safe from disaster and to bring the occupants good fortune. To achieve maximum

Ganesha, the elephant-headed god of India, the ancestor of the West's lucky elephant charm.

efficiency in this home-guarding role, the figure of the elephant had to be placed facing the front door.

The American Republican Party adopted the elephant as its symbol, presumably in the hope that it would bring the party good fortune in its campaigns.

In the 1930s, good-luck coins and 'pocket pieces' also often featured lucky elephants, but after World War II the elephant symbol slowly began to lose ground. It can still be found, but it is now far less common. There appear to be two reasons for its loss of popularity as a Body Guard. First, the elephant itself has been running out of luck in the wild. Its numbers have dwindled rapidly during the second half of the 20th century, as its habitats have shrunk. It is estimated that there are now only 40,000 Asian elephants left in the world, and most of these are in captivity. So its symbolic role as a good-luck animal seems increasingly inappropriate.

Second, through films and television we have learnt more and more about the scientific facts of elephant life. They are no longer mystical beasts, but fascinating living animals, and many people care enough about saving them to resent the idea of their being exploited in any way – even as lucky charms. Just as we now try to ban the sale of ivory, and outlaw the use of elephants in circuses, so we frown upon all forms of non-scientific thinking connected with these magnificent mammals.

Having said this, it should be mentioned that Ganesha, in his form as an elephant-headed human figure, is still extremely popular among Hindus in India. He has also been adopted by Buddhists and as a Body Guard is widely seen in the form of a small protective amulet worn around the neck.

THE PEACOCK FAN

I N INDIA IT IS a common practice to create a fan out of peacock feathers. This is kept in the house more as a protective device than as a means of keeping cool. The fans are designed so as to make maximum use of the eye markings on the feathers. It is believed that these will keep a permanent watch for any evil spirits and repel them if they come close.

In addition to the peacock fans, Indians often wear peacock feathers as part of their costume, to ward off evil. And in earlier days, those of royal rank were given the special protection of large peacock-feather umbrellas on formal occasions.

Peacock feathers are also revered in China and Japan, but the situation is reversed in the West, where they are thought to bring bad luck. There, the eye markings on the feathers are not thought to protect from the Evil Eye, but to be the Evil Eye itself. To bring even a single one into the house will lead to personal disaster.

The large peacock fan (above) captures the dramatic impact of the tail display of the bird itself.

THE PEARL

I N ONE LEGEND, a pearl is created by a drop of dew falling into a sea shell and being fertilized by the moon. In another, a white bird mates with the sun and then dives into the sea; some months later the pearl emerges. In yet another, a pearl is created by lightning striking the oyster, making it symbolic of 'the union of fire and water'.

In reality, the pearl is caused by an irritant, such as a grain of sand, entering a bivalve mollusc such as a mussel or an oyster. The mollusc, unable to eject the object, starts to build a defensive secretion around it that makes it smooth. This is the pearl.

The pearl has been employed as a protective amulet against a bewildering array of misfortunes. Worn on the body (ideally set in silver), it is reputed to: act as an aphrodisiac; relieve female depression; combat insanity; cure jaundice; purify the blood; overcome difficult objects; forecast danger; guarantee a safe journey; immunize against animal bites; improve heart conditions; protect against loss of beauty; ensure salvation; prevent early death, for a child; defend against impurity, for a bride; and, protect against sharks for a diver.

The one caution issued to wearers of pearls is that they may be seen to represent the tears of the oyster, as it suffers the pain of the rough grain of sand rasping on its soft tissues. This means that they may influence someone to 'shed many tears'. For that reason some people (especially those in love) studiously avoid wearing them.

Mother-of-pearl, the shell of the bivalve that makes pearls, is also considered, by association with the pearl, to have magical properties. Amulets made of mother-of-pearl are said to guard against evil spirits, to protect against poisoning, to heal the sick and protect a woman's virginity before marriage.

ST PAUL'S TONGUE

A protective amulet unique to the Maltese islands is the fossil shark's tooth known as the St Paul's Tongue. Still found on sale today as a decorative pendant, or lucky charm, it has been in use since medieval times and has a long and unusual history.

The St Paul's Tongue amulet is in reality the pointed tooth of a prehistoric shark.

THIS AMULET'S story begins with a ship-wreck in the year AD 60. A severe storm blew St Paul's ship onto a small island just off the coast of Malta. When St Paul was rescued and came ashore, he was bitten by a viper. His reaction was to bless the land that had saved him from drowning, and simultaneously to curse the island's snakes. As a result, all the poisonous snakes of Malta instantly lost their venom and were rendered harmless for all time.

When the snakes St Paul had cursed eventually died, they left behind a tell-tale trace in the rocks. There, just visible on the surface, were the fossilized remnants of their tongues, in the form of small, hard, triangular objects.

This story was so firmly believed that many islanders began to cut the St Paul's Tongues – which were in reality fossil shark's teeth – out of the rocks, polish them, mount them in silver or gold and attach them to necklaces or hang them from table ornaments. Because of their magical origins, these 'Tongues' were believed to provide protection against the Evil Eye and were soon being sought by wealthy families throughout the islands and beyond. The amulets' role in the legend of the 'casting out of poison' meant that they were especially important as protectors against poisoning.

In medieval times, the St Paul's Tongue amulets became part of the ritual of many banquets. At that time, royalty and noble families lived in almost constant fear of being poisoned by their enemies. This was usually done at feasts or banquets when the poisoner's actions could be concealed in the general bustle and confusion. To protect themselves against death by poisoning, the hosts developed various ways of testing their food.

One of these tests was to place a 'Viper's Teeth Tree' on the side-table that was specially set aside for the official wine-tasting. This object consisted of a tree-like ornament on which were hung a number of St Paul's Tongue amulets. In some cases, the presence alone of these sacred teeth was thought to be sufficient to remove the poison from the wine. In other instances, it was felt necessary to dip the amulets into the wine to achieve this end.

Astonishingly, almost every court in Europe between the 13th and 18th centuries employed these Maltese shark's teeth amulets to detect the presence of poison in food and drink. It was said that, in the 17th century, no ship ever left Malta without a number of the precious St Paul's Tongues on board.

After the 18th century the protective reputation of these fossil teeth waned rapidly; probably due to the discovery that the snakes of Malta have never been poisonous, and that the whole story of St Paul's curse was no more than an amusing fiction. With such revelations the magical power of the fossil teeth would soon have been discredited. However, these large teeth are remarkably beautiful fossils and their appeal has continued into the 20th century, so that, even today, they can be purchased and worn as attractive amulets, with their complex, ancient history continuing to give them a glamorous air of mystery.

This story of the St Paul's Tongue clears up one little puzzle of modern etiquette. When people order wine at a good restaurant, the waiter always pours a small amount into the glass of the host and invites them to test it. Today we imagine this is to check whether the wine is corked or not, but in reality it is a surviving relic of the old protective ritual, with the host playing the role of the taster and displaying to the guests that the wine is not poisoned.

THE OWL

The magical owl has a long history, having been sacred to Athena, the goddess of wisdom, in ancient Greece. The consequent tradition of the 'wise old owl' in folklore appears to have influenced its protective role, because its value as a lucky charm is specifically to guard against ignorance and help to increase knowledge. As an extension of this, it was thought to be 'opposed to anything that caused frenzy and unreason'.

ON THE Mediterranean island of Minorca the most popular amulet today is the owl. Made of glass or metal and hung on a cord around the neck, the image of the owl is reduced to little more than its head. Its dominant feature is a pair of staring eyes, perhaps another example of a Body Guard recruited to outstare the malevolent Evil Eye.

In the culture of this island in the Balearics, the owl appears not only as a small amulet to be worn, but also as a larger object to be placed in the house to protect its occupants from misfortune. These larger owls are usually made of white-painted ceramic, but are covered with brightly coloured details, including leaves and flowers.

It should be mentioned that the protective role of the owl is by no means universal. In many cultures, starting with ancient Rome, the bird was seen more as a demonic creature of the night, its disappearance during the daytime giving it a sinister quality that led to its being associated with witchcraft and the Devil.

Whether the owl becomes symbolically helpful or harmful in any particular instance depends on which of its characteristics are adopted for symbolic purposes. The owl appears to have an unusually large head for a bird – a head as wide as its body – and it possesses two large, front-facing eyes, whereas most birds have eyes on either side of the head. These qualities give it an air of intelligence and make it an ideal symbol of wisdom. But it also has an eerie, silent flight, a haunting cry and nocturnal habits, making it eminently suitable as a harmful symbol of witchcraft.

Why Greece should adopt a 'good owl' and Rome

The brightly coloured ceramic owl that brings good fortune to the inhabitants of Minorca.

a 'bad owl', and why today the little island of Minorca should choose the 'good owl' above all other protectors, is hard to say. It seems to be almost a matter of chance as to which of these two symbolic pathways will be taken by any particular culture.

Perhaps the strangest superstition concerning the owl is one originating from Wales which states that, if the bird is heard hooting among village houses, it means that an unmarried girl has just lost her virginity. It is interesting to speculate on just how such a strange association could begin. It seems likely that such stories arise from a misunderstanding concerning the source of the cries. In all probability, it is not the sounds made by a passing owl, but by the girl herself in her moment of truth, that are overheard by neighbours. And it is safe to assume that if there are astute myth-makers in the village, they will be able to concoct an appropriate folk-tale in order to explain events. If the sounds heard are cries of ecstasy these can be converted into the helpful hoots of a good owl, as the girl becomes wiser and more fulfilled, while if they are cries of agony they can become the harmful hoots of a bad owl, as the girl is brutally robbed of her innocence. One of the constant features of symbolic invention is its remarkable flexibility.

A small glass version of the Minorcan owl, reduced to little more than a pair of staring eyes.

THE BECKONING CAT

The most popular of all the lucky charms found in modern Japan is the **maneki neko,** *or* **Beckoning Cat.** *It is sold in huge numbers as a protective figurine. There are very small ones, to be worn on the body, and much larger ones, some more than life-size, to be placed in a vehicle or a building. It is displayed everywhere – in buses, in the home, and also in many shop windows where it invites customers to enter.*

A Japanese Beckoning Cat with its left arm raised, signifying that it is protecting a business.

THE PROTECTIVE Beckoning Cat is always shown in one specific, stylized posture – sitting upright with one of its front legs raised as if waving. It is usually made of china, though older examples are often made of wood, and is painted in traditional colours. In the most popular form, there are small black smudges on its white coat and it has a short, bobbed tail.

If worn on the body the Beckoning Cat has a double function – it attracts good luck to its owner and also wards off bad luck. Images of Beckoning Cats tied around the waist are said to protect the wearer from pain and ill-health. In the absence of an image, even the written symbol for the cat is alone considered to have protective value.

Today, those selling statuettes of the talismanic cat offer several variations on the basic theme. When purchasing a statuette, the buyer finds that it is accompanied by a piece of paper on which is written:

Thank you for buying our lucky cat. From long ago stories have been told about the lucky cat who holds up either its right or left paw, facing outward in the Japanese manner. It is beckoning, inviting customers to a business if it is raising its left paw and inviting prosperity [in the home] if it is raising its right paw. The white cat invites happiness while the gold one beckons prosperity. The black cat will beckon good health. Put a lucky cat at the entrance of houses and store windows and brighten up your day.

The legend of the origin of the Beckoning Cat is a charming one. It is told that the temple at Gotoku-ji was a very poor one, but although the monks were starving, they shared their food with their pet cat. One day the cat was sitting by the side of the road outside the temple, when a group of rich samurai rode up. The cat beckoned to them and they followed it into the temple.

As soon as the samurai had entered the building, a terrible rainstorm arrived. A bolt of lightning struck the ground exactly where the samurai had been standing just before they followed the cat into the temple. The cat had therefore saved their lives, for which they were immensely grateful. The heavy rain forced them to shelter for quite a while and they passed the time learning about the Buddhist philosophy. Later, one of the samurai returned to take religious instruction and eventually endowed the temple with a large estate. His family were buried there, and near their tombs a small cat-shrine was built to the memory of the Beckoning Cat.

The temple in question still exists, but today it has been swallowed up by the western suburbs of Tokyo. Despite this, it remains a popular centre for those who wish to pray for their cats, and the cat-shrine is regularly festooned with offerings. The cat breed known as the Japanese Bobtail is now closely identified with the legendary Beckoning Cat, and it is thought that to own one will bring good luck.

Some authors record a completely different legend to explain the popularity of the Beckoning Cat. According to this tale, a famous woman in Yoshiwara was about to be attacked by a dangerous snake. Her favourite cat saw the danger and tried to warn her by raising its paw, but was killed in the attempt. She had an effigy of the cat carved in wood, and copies then became popular as lucky charms, to protect their owners from danger.

China has its own version of the talismanic feline, the Silkworm Cat. Images of this cat were placed on the walls of the houses of Chinese silkworm breeders to protect their silkworms from harm during the breeding season. It was believed that the pictures would have the power to frighten off the rats that often plagued the farmers.

THE HORNS

The protective act of placing a pair of bull's horns on the roof or wall of a building can be traced back at least 8,000 years to the neolithic period, a time, thousands of years ago, when the great horned god was all powerful.

ONE OF THE EARLIEST towns known to archaeology, Çatal Hüyük in Anatolia (part of modern Turkey), which was inhabited from around 6250 BC, was found to have buildings that contained rooms that were decorated with horns. In fact, horned artefacts appear repeatedly right through the Bronze Age and the Iron Age in many places in the Middle East and around the Mediterranean.

To ancient people the bull was a symbol of power, because of its size and savagery; a symbol of animal fertility, because of its impressive mating acts; and a symbol of crop fertility, because of the way the ox-plough opened up the earth for the early farmers. Converted into a horned god, the bull was the ideal protector of men, livestock and crops. The massive horns of this Great Protector became his emblem, his guardian sign. It was enough simply to make the horn-sign with the fingers of the hand, to invoke his protection. But holding the hand in that position was inevitably a fleeting gesture, and so a more permanent object was needed to give protection to buildings that were in constant danger from evil spirits.

The solution was to take the real horns from a bull's skull, or to fashion horns from some other material, and fix them in a high, conspicuous position, facing defiantly outwards, challenging the unseen and the unknown. Such horns can be seen to this day on the island of Malta, where many of the old farmhouses are adorned with one or more pairs, either real or sculptured. The occupants of these buildings today may be devout Christians, but when faced with the threat of the Evil Eye they still rely on the much earlier, pagan horned god to defend them from harm.

In addition to protecting buildings, horns have been worn on the body in many cultures. Warriors have frequently donned a horned helmet to strike fear into the enemy camp. This is not because it is possible to attack physically with the points of the horns, or because they give the wearer any concrete protection, but because the mere sight of them is so threatening. They give the warrior the look of a powerful animal and magically endow him with the bull's great strength.

In modern Italy protective horns are also frequently encountered as pendants. Usually made of gold or silver, they take the form of an elegant, small, single horn, hanging from a chain around the neck, and are seen as symbols of male virility and sexual potency.

A pair of bull's horns protecting a Maltese farmhouse and its occupants from the Evil Eye, a pagan relic in a Catholic country.

THE COWRIE

The cowrie shell is one of the most ancient of all Body Guards, having been placed in tombs in prehistoric times to protect the dead. Its use as an amulet dates back over 20,000 years. There are two quite distinct symbolic interpretations for these small marine shells.

As a protective amulet, the cowrie shell is the most popular of all molluscs, playing a role in human adornment all over the world.

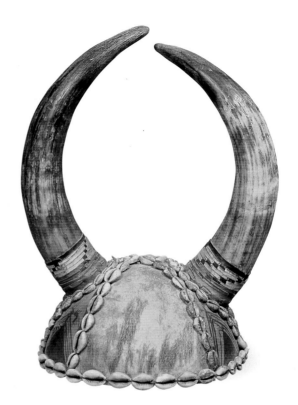

The cowrie as an eye

The first interpretation sees cowries as eyes, used to outstare the Evil Eye. With a little imagination, their ovoid shape does resemble the visible part of the human eye. In this capacity they were sometimes placed in the eye-sockets of corpses, giving them permanent, non-rotting eyes to provide new sight in the afterlife. This custom was widespread and has been traced in regions as varied as Egypt, West Africa, Borneo and New Zealand.

In Nigeria, ceremonial headdresses often incorporated large numbers of cowrie shells, creating a sea of staring eyes, gazing in all directions. The example shown here (above right) boasts no fewer than 106 cowries.

In India, Iran and Egypt, cowries were attached to the trappings of elephants, horses and camels to protect these essential beasts of burden from attacks by the Evil Eye. Also, in India, the most valuable cattle had cowries tied to their necks or placed on their foreheads for the same purpose. The cowrie's popularity in India is thought to have given it its modern name, the word 'cowrie' probably having come from the name 'Kauri' – the title of a pre-Vedic (1500–800 BC) goddess.

The cowrie as female genitals

The second interpretation sees the aperture in the cowrie shell as the genital slit of the human female. In earlier writings the cowrie shell was sometimes referred to as representing 'the female gate of life'. In this capacity, the cowrie became a potent fertility symbol and, as a treasured amulet, a protector against infertility and painful childbirth.

In this sexual role the cowrie symbol has been traced to the South Pacific, the Middle East and much of the Mediterranean rim. In Japan it was once the custom for a woman to hold a cowrie shell in her hand when she was giving birth, in order to ensure an easy delivery. And in several cultures it was a common practice for girls to wear cowries fixed to their skirts as a way of encouraging pregnancy. Because of their association with fertility, cowries were often placed in tombs to increase the chances of rebirth in the afterlife.

In ancient Egypt it was especially popular. In predynastic times, over 5,000 years ago, sexual cowries were represented by the actual shells themselves, but later, about 4,000 years ago, they were being fashioned in blue-glazed pottery, in cornelian and in quartz. Before long there were also precious cowrie ornaments made of gold or silver. The favourite place for wearing these amulets was the female girdle, in this way locating them close to the source of their symbolic origins.

THE FROG

Frog amulets were popular in ancient Egypt, usually made of gold, blue faience or steatite. They were thought to protect against loss of virility and against infertility. Because huge numbers of little frogs could be seen suddenly emerging from the water, Egyptians associated them with the renewal of life and fecundity. Frog amulets were sometimes placed on mummies to assist them in finding rebirth.

THE EARLY Christians observed with interest the way in which tadpoles turned into adult frogs. They also noted the way adult frogs, after burying themselves in the ground for long periods of time, magically re-emerged and 'returned to life'. Inevitably this made the small amphibians ideal subjects to represent the idea of resurrection. The image of a frog was sometimes shown next to the Coptic cross, drawing a parallel between the metamorphosis of the frog and the rising of Christ from the dead.

During Roman times, a frog amulet was thought to protect a house and its occupants from misfortune. And, because a frog was 'born from foam' like Venus, the Romans believed that wearing a frog amulet could prevent the loss of love.

Later on, in the Middle Ages, the dried body of a frog was sometimes worn in a small silk bag around the neck, as a protection against fits. This reverence for the frog was in stark contrast to attitudes towards the poisonous toad, which was seen as an associate of the Devil and of witches.

A metal frog amulet sold today as a lucky charm in parts of the Middle East.

Today, like some other animal Body Guards, the frog has largely lost its protective flavour, but frog amulets do still exist. Some people wear a small, carved frog as a pendant on a necklace, or a brooch near the heart, to guard against bad feelings between friends. And there is a Chinese Moon Frog talisman, available even in the Western world, which is worn around the neck to ensure longevity and wealth. (The reason it is linked to the moon is that, like the moon, the frog changes its shape during the phases of its life.) Sometimes a statue of the Chinese Moon Frog is seen with an old coin placed in its mouth, which is because old Chinese coins are employed as guardians to ward off evil.

An ancient Roman frog amulet, depicted on a 1920s cigarette card.

For some reason, a frog amulet carved from amber has been popular for many years in Italy, Greece and Turkey. It is worn in those countries as a lucky charm to bring its owners good health, prosperity and an abundance of earthly riches.

A Chinese frog amulet worn as a pendant to ensure a long life and great riches.

THE SEA SHELL

S HELLS HAVE BEEN used as amulets for thousands of years and in many parts of the world, from Asia to the South Pacific and from the Middle East to tropical Africa. In some cases they have been found in regions far removed from the sea, indicating that considerable effort was sometimes involved in transporting them to the places where they were highly valued.

A tiny bivalve mollusc amulet worn today as a fertility charm.

When bivalves were involved, they were nearly always associated with female sexuality. Terms used included 'the life-giving female', sexual passion, female genitals, fertility, birth and love. The link to sexual passion was based on the way the two halves of the bivalve shell cling tightly to one another. The link to birth and the 'life-giving female' was based on the way the shell opens, revealing the soft interior. In one famous folklore tradition, depicted in a Botticelli painting (*The Birth of Venus*, in the Uffizi Gallery in Florence), the goddess of love was born from an opening scallop shell.

The talismanic conch shell is encountered in both Buddhist and Hindu contexts. In Buddhism it symbolizes the voice of Buddha. For Hindus it is sacred to Vishnu and symbolizes the call to awaken from ignorance. As a charm, it has been associated with oratory and learning and to protect against misfortune and poverty.

The most widespread shell amulet is based on the cowrie (see page 36).

THE SPIDER

I N ENGLAND A small spider appearing in the home is often referred to as a Money Spider, a Money-spinner or a Money-maker. If one crawls into view, hangs from a thread, lands on a table or walks over a hand, it is carefully moved to safety. If it is destroyed, money will be lost; if it survives, riches will be gained. A spider amulet carries the same message. Such amulets, made of gold or silver, were common in ancient Rome, when they were worn to bring success in trade.

Curiously, on the other side of the world, in Polynesia, there is a similar tradition, namely that if a small spider lowers itself on a thread in front of you, you will receive a valuable present – a gift from heaven. In parts of the United States it is also believed that it is unlucky to kill a spider and that, if you do so, you will suffer from bad weather. In many countries it is believed that, if a large house-spider shares your room, you will enjoy great prosperity and happiness. These pro-spider traditions have given rise to a popular saying: 'If you wish to live and thrive, let the spider run alive.'

There is an ancient legend that establishes the idea of the spider as a great protector. It is said that when the infant Jesus (or King David, or Mohammed, or Frederick the Great – according to the allegiance of the storyteller) was hiding from soldiers in a cave, a spider wove a conspicuous web across the entrance. When the soldiers arrived they assumed that nobody could have passed through the entrance for some time and moved on without bothering to search the inside of the cave.

In several Native American tribes an artificial spider's web is fashioned and hung over a baby's cradle to 'catch its bad dreams' and spirit them away. These webs are called 'dreamcatchers' (see page 196).

Many people hate spiders, but others see them as protectors and wear images of them as small pendants.

41

RED CORAL

Branching red coral, sometimes referred to as the 'Tree of Life of the Ocean' – has been employed in the making of amulets for many centuries. It is sometimes used in a natural form (when it is supposed to be most effective as a protective device), or it may be fashioned into beads, pendants, brooches or necklaces.

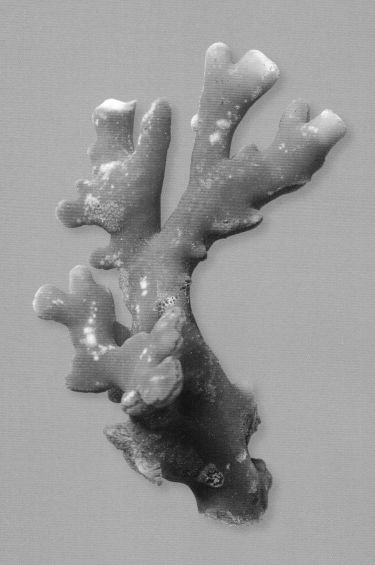

A 1496 painting of the Madonna, with a large branch of protective red coral hanging above her head.

ACCORDING to ancient Greek legend, when the hero Perseus cut off the head of the terrible Medusa, whose look would turn a man to stone, the monster's blood gushed out and, falling into the sea, grew into beautiful red coral. For this reason, sailors and fishermen, in particular, feel that to carry a small piece of red coral will protect them from the hazards of the ocean. To this day, many Italian fishermen refuse to go out to sea without this particular form of Body Guard on their person.

Among the supposed powers of a red-coral amulet is protection from the Evil Eye, from demons, from the magic spells of witches, from lunacy and from all forms of disease. It was also seen as a powerful defence against sterility because it symbolized the fertility of water – the water that could grow beautiful red 'gems' from the blood of a slaughtered monster.

Women wore a red-coral amulet to protect them from hormonal irregularities and, when pregnant, were encouraged to place one near their genitals. This was believed to ensure an easy delivery.

Red coral was especially popular as a protector of babies, and it was once a common practice for an infant's nanny to fasten a coral amulet around her baby's neck before taking the child out in

The addition of red coral to items of jewellery is thought to give them protective qualities.

public. It was said to be especially effective when the baby was teething.

Belief in the power of red coral was such that it became a multi-purpose protector. In addition to its use in portable amulets, it was also employed in various other ways:

♣ Hung up in the home to protect against evil influences
♣ Hung on the bedpost to protect against nocturnal terrors
♣ Placed among the roof rafters to protect against lightning
♣ Attached to the mast of a ship to protect against storms and shipwreck
♣ Tied to fruit-trees to protect against poor fruit-bearing
♣ Placed among crops to protect against plagues of locusts
♣ Sewn up in a dog's collar to protect against rabies.

THE WISHBONE

The lucky wishbone is the U-shaped collarbone of a chicken (or, at Christmas, a turkey).

In the West it has for many years been a popular custom to save this bone after a chicken

or turkey has been eaten and then use it in a small 'good-luck' ritual. The full ritual

consists of drying the bone for three days until it is brittle. It is then known by the name

'merrythought' and is given to two people to pull apart.

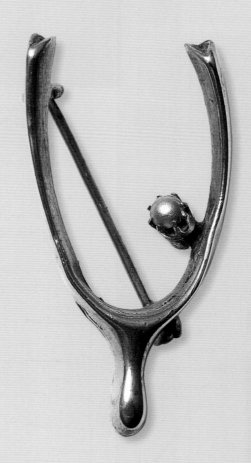

THE PULLING OF A wishbone should be done in a special way, with each contestant holding one end of the bone by crooking a little finger around it. At a given signal they both start to pull the bone towards themselves. As the pressure on the bone increases, it breaks in two, but never at its strong centre-point. Instead it snaps into two unequal parts and the winner is the one left holding the longer section. This winner is then able to make a wish which, it is claimed, will come true only if it is kept secret. This full ritual is rarely enacted today. Instead, two people enjoying a meal simply grasp the wishbone as soon as it has been stripped of meat and, holding it in any way they like, snap it apart.

The most popular time for wishbone-wishing is the Christmas holiday, when large birds feature so conspicuously on the dining table. In the north of England there has been a long tradition that if a young unmarried woman should be lucky enough to obtain the wishbone during the Christmas celebrations, she should not share it and break it, but keep it carefully and hang it over the doorway of her home. If she puts it up on New Year's Day, it is predicted that the first man to enter her house will become her husband. In other words, she can use the wishbone as a form of fertility charm. In this role, the fact that its shape is reminiscent of a horseshoe is significant. Indeed, there are some who

The wishbone is rather rare as a protective amulet, but occasionally appears as a motif on a small brooch.

believe that the wishbone's power stems solely from the way its U-shape echoes that of the lucky horseshoe.

Others paint a different picture of the superstitious origins of the wishbone, relating it instead to ancient oracles. Hens were once thought to be able to foretell the future, and ceremonies were carried out in which carefully arranged grains of corn represented the letters of the alphabet. When the hen pecked at the corn it spelled out magical words, after which the unfortunate bird was sacrificed. The wishbone was cut from its corpse, cleaned and dried and was then held by the person who wanted to make a wish for some particular kind of good fortune.

It is possible today to obtain a small wishbone amulet in either gold or silver, which is usually worn as a brooch. It was also found as an image on some North American good-luck coins in the 1930s. Perhaps because it is a 'dead animal part', it is now fading in popularity in the increasingly prevalent climate of greater respect for animal life. Eventually its only legacy may be the phrase 'lucky break', which is taken from the idea that the person who breaks off the larger portion of the bone will be the one who gets the good luck.

A wishbone is sometimes carefully kept and fixed on a wall as a lucky charm instead of being snapped in two.

THE ADDER STONE

The legend of St Hilda tells how she drove away the venomous snakes that infested the grassland where she wished to build her abbey, near the clifftops of Whitby. By using special prayers and magic spells she made the serpents curl up into tight spirals and roll over the cliffs on to the beach below. As they perished they emitted saliva which turned them into fossils. For centuries their fossilized remains have been used as protective amulets.

I N REALITY, THE fossils still found on the Whitby beaches to this day are not snakes but prehistoric molluscs. They are ammonites, which happen to be particularly common in that region. The largest ones are too big to be worn, or carried in a purse or pocket, but they can be used as garden or house guards. The smallest ones are tiny enough to be mounted and worn as a pendant. Before selling them today, the local people 'improve' them by adding a snake's head at the end of the shell-spiral.

The adder, or viper, is the only venomous snake to be found in England, so if in the Middle Ages there really were hordes of venomous snakes in the long grass of Whitby, they must have been adders, which is how the amulet made from this type of fossil acquired the name Adder Stone. Alternative names are Snake Stone and St Hilda's Stone. There is an interesting parallel between this legend and the one in which St Paul banishes the venomous snakes of Malta from the island (see pages 28–9).

Because of their legendary connection with snakes, these small ammonites have often been used to protect country people from adder-bites. There are from Victorian times records of local 'wise-women' being summoned to the bedside of some-one suffering from a painful snake-bite. Once there, the 'wise-woman' would rub her 'Snake Stone' on the swollen flesh, where the snake's fangs struck, and in no time at all the swelling would subside. (The truth is that British adder-bites are rarely severe for human beings and the swelling soon disappears of its own accord, with or without the help of ammonites.)

As powerful amulets Adder Stones have also been used to protect people from a variety of illnesses such as fever, whooping cough and eye diseases. They have also been used for the prevention of nightmares. When this power is being sought they are hung above the bed at night, like Native American Indian dreamcatchers (see page 196).

This fossil ammonite is easily converted into an Adder Stone by carving a small head on it (see opposite page).

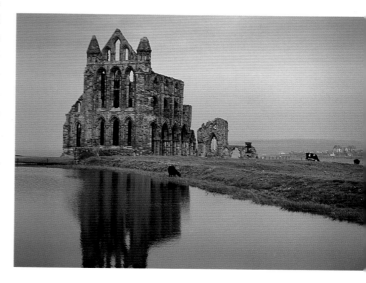

St Hilda, a seventh-century abbess, built her abbey near the clifftops of Whitby on the north-eastern coast of England.

HORSE HORNS

HORSES WITH HORNS may sound like a zoological contradiction, but on the island of Malta the horses that pull the antique carriages called *karrozzin* do wear a pair of miniature metal horns on their heads. The horns fit on top of a strap that is part of the bridle and offer the horse the same protection as the full-sized ones that adorn so many of the Maltese farm-buildings.

They invoke the power of the ancient horned god of pre-Christian times. It was this pagan deity, originally the great protector of his devout followers, that became demonized by the Christian Church and converted into their great enemy, the Devil. In a country as passionately Christian as Malta is today, it is amusing to find these early forms of superstition still practised so seriously.

The horns, whose magical task is to protect the horse from evil spirits, are decorated with a large, central, vertical feather, usually from a peacock or a pheasant. This feather acts as an additional Body Guard. If it is from a peacock's tail, its bold eye marking is seen as outstaring the Evil Eye.

In most of Europe this feather is thought to bring bad luck, and it is only much farther to the east that it becomes a lucky motif. The Shah of Persia, for example, sat on a peacock throne, and in India the eye of the peacock feather is ever on the watch for approaching danger (see page 26).

Sometimes a further protective device is attached to the horns – a (fake) ruby. This gem, with its centuries-old reputation for protecting the wearer from injury, is presumably there to look after the physical well-being of the animal.

On the island of Malta the horses that pull the carriages are protected from evil by a small pair of metal horns.

THE LADYBIRD

THE SMALL RED beetle with black spots, known as the ladybird or ladybug, enjoys an international popularity that seems out of proportion to its modest appearance. In addition to the ladybird or ladybug it is also referred to as Lady Beetle, God Almighty's Cow, the Bird of Our Lady and the Beetle of Our Lady. In France it is the Poulette à Dieu ('God's Little Chicken'); in Italy the Palomilla; in Germany the Marienkäfer; in Spain the Mariquita.

In the Middle Ages the ladybird was dedicated to the Virgin Mary. It has since acquired a worldwide reputation as a good-luck symbol, and harming or killing one is said to bring very bad luck. The traditional response to seeing one land nearby is to chant the rhyme 'Ladybird, ladybird, fly away home, your house is on fire, your children will burn'.

Instead of suffering the usual fate of an insect and being squashed or swatted, the little beetle is then encouraged to fly away unharmed. This is fortunate because it happens to be a useful species that preys upon garden insect pests.

Because of the folklore attached to it, the ladybird is believed to bring great success and riches to those who wear it as an amulet. If worn by those who are sick, it is believed to absorb the illness and then to spirit it away.

Like the stork, the ladybird is a child-bringer and in some regions the number of black spots on its back is said to indicate the number of children a woman will have. This superstition effectively converts the ladybird into a fertility amulet.

The fame of the ladybird as a good-luck symbol has spread to many countries.

OTHER ANIMAL AMULETS

IN ADDITION TO the major animal amulets, there are a number of minor ones.

Butterfly

It is perhaps surprising that the butterfly, which in the adult form lives for only a few days, should have come to represent longevity and immortality. Its gentle flight and its beauty have, however, made it into a symbol of the soul and therefore of eternal life.

Cat

The cat is seen as lucky in some countries and unlucky in others. In ancient Egypt it was sacred, and thousands of cat amulets have been found in excavations there. In medieval times, the Christian Church decreed that the cat was a servant of the Devil, and its use as an amulet disappeared. Later still, a superstition arose that, if you see a black cat and the devil does not strike you down, you must be very lucky. So, in this roundabout way, the black cat once again became associated with good luck, and people began wearing black-cat brooches. Some countries, even today, however, still take the view that to wear such an amulet would bring bad luck.

Deer

Presumably because of its spectacular rutting habits, the deer has become a symbol of sexuality. Amulets made from deer antlers or hooves are said to protect against infertility and other sexual problems.

Dolphin

Popular among sailors, the dolphin has been used as an amulet to protect against dangers at sea.

Dove

A symbol of peace and the Holy Spirit, the dove has often been worn as an amulet, especially in times of strife and war. It is said to offer protection against death, fire, lightning and a loveless life.

Dragon

In China, the sacred Celestial Dragon is a symbol of courage, vigilance and security, a mystical creature of supreme spirituality. As an amulet, even today, it is popular as a guard against unhappiness, infertility, and the loss of love.

Egg

The egg is an obvious symbol of fertility, but is seldom worn as an amulet despite its reputation. Each year at Easter, the giving and eating of chocolate eggs is a cheerful reminder of the time when their role as protective amulets was taken more seriously.

Feather

A golden feather was an important amulet in ancient Egypt to bring wealth and prosperity.

This lucky black-cat brooch comes from the Isle of Man, home of the famous tailless Manx breed.

Fox

A fox amulet is considered helpful for apprentice shape-shifters, and as a defence against poverty. The tail of a fox was sometimes carried as a Body Guard to increase speed and cunning.

Goat

Goat amulets have always been used to increase sexual potency and protect against infertility.

Grasshopper

Farmers sometimes carry a little green grasshopper amulet to protect them from poor harvests.

Lamb

The lamb has for centuries been viewed as a symbol of Jesus Christ. As such, its image protects those who wear it from infertility and brings them peace.

Lion

A symbol of strength, bravery, honour, health, wealth and success, the lion amulet is thought to be valuable to those undertaking dangerous journeys.

Ram

Popular in ancient Egypt and still in use today, with its powerful charge, the ram is a favourite of sportsmen. For women, it is a symbol of fertility.

Scorpion

A scorpion amulet is supposed to protect the wearer against all forms of evil, especially attacks.

Swallow

A swallow nesting under the roof is thought to bring good luck, a superstition that has sometimes led to the wearing of a small silver swallow amulet.

Tortoise/turtle

The land-living tortoise and its close relative the sea-dwelling turtle have appeared as protective beings in several mythologies. The most famous legend sees the tortoise as the symbol of eternal life, supporting the entire world on its back. This 'cosmic turtle' or tortoise became a symbol of longevity, wisdom, strength, stability, fortitude, benevolence and patience and was worn as a defence against sudden death, ignorance, rash decisions and other weaknesses. A turtle amulet fashioned from gold was also said to offer protection from loss of creativity and compassion. Cups made from tortoiseshell are believed to protect the drinker from poisoning, and tortoiseshell bracelets are worn as a defence against evil and black magic.

Unicorn

An amulet in the shape of a unicorn's long, single horn is supposed to provide protection against loss of chastity. Seemingly contradicting this, it also helps to guard against infertility and sexual inadequacy, and it has also been used to detect poisons.

Rock of Ages
MINERAL BODY GUARDS

In an age where so many of the traditional magic symbols are no longer 'ethically correct', especially those with animal origins, many people are seeking a 'clean' form of magic. And nothing could be cleaner or less connected with taboo subjects such as 'dead animal parts' than pure metals, crystals or gems. As a result, recent years have seen a resurgence of interest in mineral amulets and lucky charms. New Age centres are spreading like wildfire, offering a huge variety of stones and crystals that can be worn as pendants and brooches, or simply carried in a bag or pocket. Each type of geological specimen is said to possess certain specific healing or protective properties, often associated with particular birth signs.

THE STONES

BECAUSE OF THEIR rarity and their beauty, crystals and unusual stones and rocks have for centuries been used as magic amulets. In fact, almost all forms of jewellery began as protective Body Guards. Whether as rings, pendants, necklaces, bracelets, anklets, crowns or brooches, the earliest examples of the jeweller's art were worn to bring their owners good luck or to ward off evil spirits.

The gleaming gems in a king's crown were there, not merely to proclaim his dominant role, but also to guard him against a whole range of hostile supernatural forces and occult misfortunes. From the primitive stone juju charms of the tribal witch-doctors to the most elaborate adornments of the royal courts, early jewels were, almost without exception, seen as devices for overcoming the mysterious, evil influences that were so feared by the intensely superstitious minds of earlier centuries.

Little by little, this original, ancient purpose was replaced by two other considerations – beauty and status. As the jewellers' skills grew and their techniques improved, their creations increasingly became great works of art. They were enjoyed, not because of their magical powers, but simply because they looked so exquisite. Aesthetics ousted superstition as the main driving force behind bodily adornment. And because these complex new creations were so expensive, they became important symbols of high status. In a few instances the old, superstitious significance of a particular type of jewellery managed to survive, but for the most part it was lost.

The scientific explanations of modern mineralogy began to erode the earlier beliefs, but by this time the traditions of beautiful jewellery were sufficiently entrenched for it to survive on other grounds. Today, however, in a modern revolt against scientific thought, brought on no doubt by the many misuses of science that have blighted the modern environment, many people are now reverting to the earlier, mystical belief-systems. The magical use of crystals has once again become popular and many are now on sale as occult objects to be employed in the old ways. The transition between the old and new millenniums is bringing a strange

Crystals, rocks, stones, gems and pebbles have for centuries provided the raw materials for many different kinds of Body Guards.

resurgence in belief in the protective powers of minerals. The younger generation is once again wearing crystals and gems for non-decorative, non-status reasons. A new era of mineral magic has dawned.

Some people find it astonishing that something as dramatically, transparently inorganic as a crystal should be endowed with obscure, mystical powers. But perhaps it is precisely because their structure and appearance offer such a vivid contrast to the irregular softness of most biological forms that they have acquired their special appeal. Although very much a part of nature, their shiny, geometric surfaces somehow seem to belong to another world. Nothing could be further from mud and slush, or from earth and grass, than a gleaming crystal. It is almost as if it has come from another planet. And, in a modern era where things change more quickly than ever before, the permanence of crystals and rocks provides for some a sense of security and comfort.

One reason for the special appeal and magical power of stones and crystals is the idea that a cut and prepared crystal is like a human being with the rough animal exterior removed to reveal the gleaming soul beneath. Another explanation is the concept of the mystical 'state of transparency', in which the cut crystal is seen as a presentation of opposites

– the stone exists because it is hard to the touch, but it does not exist because we can see right through it. It is solid to the hand but liquid to the eye. A third possible reason is that certain crystals are said to possess inside them an occult force, rather like a magnetic field, which can influence the condition of those in contact with them.

When a mineral is employed as a protective amulet or as a decorative ornament and appreciated for its beauty, it is referred to as a 'gem'. The value of a particular kind of gem is based not only on its colour and its rarity, but also especially on its hardness. It is this quality that gives it its 'strength' and durability. There is a simple scale of gem hardness (the Mohs Scale), with diamond at the top scoring 10. Others are ranked according to which will scratch which. Some of the best known gems are as follows: diamond – 10; ruby and sapphire – 9; emerald, aquamarine and topaz – 8; garnet and quartz – 7; agate, jade and moonstone – 6 to 7; hematite, lapis lazuli, opal and turquoise – 5 to 6; malachite – 3 to 4.

Each type of gem is believed to have its own special, protective influences, and large numbers of them have been endowed, or perhaps one should say 're-endowed', with some kind of supernatural power. The main types of gem that are involved are covered on the following pages.

AMETHYST

Amethyst derives its name (which comes from the Greek and means 'without intoxication') from the idea that, if an amulet made from this distinctive purple stone was worn to a celebration or a party, the wearer would be protected from drunkenness. This strange belief made amethysts extremely popular in both ancient Egypt and ancient Greece.

ARISTOTLE EXPLAINS THE mysterious association between this attractive gem and a state of sobriety in the following way. During a drunken orgy, Dionysus, the god of wine, seized a beautiful young nymph called Amethyst with the intention of ravishing her. She quickly prayed to the goddess of chastity to save her and was promptly transformed into a gleaming jewel in Bacchus' horny hands. Understandably, this sobered him up in an instant and made him feel deeply ashamed. To atone, he gave the gleaming stone the beautiful pale-purple colour of his favourite wine and swore that, from that day onwards, anyone wearing such a stone would be protected from his drunken ways.

A completely different and much less fanciful explanation is given by another ancient legend, which tells of an attempted poisoning. The deadly poison was placed in a cup fashioned out of amethyst and when the intended victim drank from this cup, the poison had no effect.

It was concluded thereafter that anyone in contact with amethyst would be immune to the effects of any drink.

The magical ability to absorb alcohol from the bloodstream is only one of amethyst's many occult powers. In its other capacities it is known by a variety of names, including the Bishop's Stone, the Beneficent Stone, the Elevator, the Stone of Healing, the Stone of Peace and the Stone of Love. In its role as the Elevator, it should prevent loss of energy. As the Stone of Healing, it is supposed to protect against weakness in the immune system. Wishful thinkers also claim that carrying it on the body will guard against neuralgia, blood clots and cancers. As the Stone of Peace, it is thought to defend against stress and violence, to calm fears, to cure hysteria and, when taken to bed, to defeat insomnia. In earlier centuries it was also said to defend the wearer against thieves. As the Stone of Love – worn constantly, so it is said, by St Valentine – it is reputed to be one of the best gifts between lovers.

It is claimed that an amethyst key-ring, like this one from Brazil, will protect party-goers from drunkenness.

OPAL

THE OPAL, KNOWN as the Rainbow Stone, has a mixed reputation and is avoided by many people. Its brittle texture and variable colour mean that it is unsuitable as a symbol of constancy and is therefore inappropriate for use as an amulet by lovers or spouses.

Some authorities insist that the opal is a bad-luck stone for everyone, but this is not generally accepted. In fact, the name opal comes from the Sanskrit word *upala*, meaning 'Valued Stone'. It is often worn as a protection against lack of confidence and against actions by enemies. Furthermore, it has the reputation of a gem that absorbs negative feelings and guards against depression, apathy and stress.

In a different capacity, it has been said to be effective against eye diseases and to sharpen the eyesight. As a result, it is sometimes referred to as the 'Eye Stone' or the 'Eye of the World'. It also has a reputation for increasing hope, as this Victorian verse confirms: 'October's child is born for woe, and life's vicissitudes must know, but lay an opal on her breast, and hope will lull those woes to rest.'

Opal is obviously one of the slightly contradictory stones. On the one hand it is said to protect the wearer from a whole range of calamities, while on the other hand it is considered by many to curse its owner with misfortune. In Sir Walter Scott's novel *Anne of Geierstein* (1829), misfortune befalls the owner of an opal. It has been suggested that many of its supposed negative qualities stem from that source, though it is possible that Scott was only using a reputation he was familiar with from elsewhere.

There is, however, another source that also does little to boost its reputation. An old Australian legend describes the opal as a half-human, half-serpent devil who lurks beneath the surface of the earth, ready to lure men to their doom with 'flashes of evil magic'. This sounds like a story invented by an old rock-hunter who, on a bad day, has fallen down a hole. Be that as it may, it has certainly not improved the occult status of this particular type of stone. And the story itself makes it a great mystery why Australia should have chosen the brittle, ambivalent opal as its national stone.

QUARTZ

OMETIMES CALLED THE Stone of Power, the quartz crystal has been central to magical and healing rituals for centuries, and has been widely employed as an amulet against all forms of evil influence. The author of a recent volume on the metaphysical aspects of crystals devoted no fewer than 52 pages to its protective and healing properties.

In particular it is believed to guard against loss of vitality and strength. There are also claims that it is a great aid to mental concentration, which explains its traditional use by clairvoyants, in the form of large crystal balls.

Clear quartz is also known traditionally as Rock Crystal, but there are several other varieties. Rose quartz is called the Love Stone. This pale pink quartz is said to protect the wearer from anger, guilt, fear and jealousy, and it also acts as a Body Guard against infertility. Worn when you are alone, it is said to relieve feelings of tension, sadness and isolation.

Milky quartz is an opaque white variety. This has been central to magical and healing rituals for centuries, and has been widely employed as a protective amulet against all forms of evil influence. Again, like clear quartz, it is believed to protect against loss of vitality.

Smoky quartz is a darker variety, known as the Dream Stone and is reputed to protect against despair, grief, anger, depression and other forms of negativity. It also has a strong reputation as a healing stone and is said to be especially helpful in dealing with unpleasant wounds.

Quartz is increasingly worn as a small crystal pendant to aid in mental concentration.

LODESTONE

THIS DARK, HEAVY, highly magnetic stone has been used in mystical ways for many centuries. In ancient Egypt there was once a plan to make the entire roof of a temple, dedicated to Arsinoe, from this material, so that the goddess below would become magically suspended in mid-air beneath the massive magnetic pull of the roof. Unfortunately the architect died before his imaginative theory could be put to the test.

Because lodestone (also known as magnetite) would attract objects to it, it was thought to be an effective amulet for loving couples, increasing their attraction for one another. For this reason it was frequently used in wedding rings. In China it is known as t'su shi, the Loving Stone. In ancient Assyria, men and women would rub a lodestone over their bodies before making love. And in Mexico it is said to be favoured by prostitutes, presumably to act as a magnet for new customers.

It was also employed as a protection against infidelity. If there were dark suspicions that a loved one was being unfaithful, all that was necessary was to hide a lodestone under her pillow. If she had indeed been disloyal, the presence of the stone would make her fall out of bed. ('If polluted by adultery found, hurled from the couch she tumbles to the ground.') If she did not react in this way, then the suspicions were completely unfounded. It is not hard to guess whether this superstition was first invented by a faithful or an unfaithful partner.

If there is any truth in the theory that small changes in magnetic fields can influence the behaviour or condition of the human body, then it is possible that lodestone has a genuine impact on those who wear it as an amulet, an impact that is scientifically precise rather than supernaturally vague. We do know that complex responses to changes in magnetic fields occur in homing birds so perhaps it is not too fanciful to suggest that something similar may take place with our own species. Having said this, it must be admitted that carrying a lodestone as an amulet would be more likely to disrupt delicate magnetic responses than to amplify them. But at this stage of our knowledge we cannot be sure.

MALACHITE

GREEN MALACHITE HAS been employed as a protective amulet for infants. Attached to their cradles, it was believed to keep evil spirits away and allow the babies to sleep peacefully. It was said that the swirling patterns in the green stone were especially valuable at repelling the Evil Eye. Worn or carried, malachite is believed to soothe the wearer and defeat depression.

In apparent contradiction to this, some authors have suggested that malachite contains mysterious powers that mean the stone can itself be used as an Evil Eye. This contradiction no doubt stems from the fact that the natural patterns in the stone have been likened to those on the peacock's tail. In Italy this led to its being called the Peacock Stone. The peacock's magical reputation varies enormously from country to country. In some regions it is beneficial and protects against evil. In others it is evil itself. It would seem that malachite has inherited this duality from the exotic bird.

There is always the possibility, of course, that those who placed malachite amulets on their babies' cradles were well aware of this duality and that they were simply setting their own outward-looking Evil Eye to defeat another, incoming one – a case of an eye for an eye.

Polished Malachite eggs from Africa, displaying the patterns of dark and light green that give this stone its special appeal.

BLOODSTONE

BLOODSTONE IS A DARK green stone marked with flecks of red. Small pieces of it were considered to be powerful amulets in ancient Egypt, where legend associated it with the great protective goddess Isis. Referred to as the Blood of Isis, it was often placed in the tomb to protect the deceased. In life, it was considered an exceptionally useful amulet for women, protecting them from menstrual problems and difficulties during pregnancy and birth.

Christianity took over the 'Blood of Isis' and converted it into the 'Blood of Christ'. The flecks of

A star-shaped bloodstone, still worn as an amulet today, especially as a protection against stress.

red in the green stone became spots of Christ's blood, shed onto the rocks of Calvary following the thrust of the Roman soldier's spear into Christ's body as He hung on the cross.

Bloodstone was especially popular among Roman gladiators and Roman soldiers, who carried bloodstone amulets with them into battle to protect them from loss of blood if they were wounded. And both Roman and Greek athletes wore bloodstone talismans to assist them in the Games.

Although it has lost some of its earlier glamour, bloodstone remains moderately popular today and is still believed to protect the wearer from a variety of misfortunes, especially problems connected with blood, such as haemorrhage, 'tired blood' and other circulatory disorders. It is also supposed to protect against stress, lack of self-belief and to help its owners to develop special abilities and talents. According to a Victorian verse, the bloodstone is especially protective to those born in March, recommending that it would be wise 'in days of peril firm and brave, to wear a Bloodstone to their grave'.

CITRINE

S OMETIMES CALLED THE Cuddle Quartz, citrine is thought to be able to prevent low self-esteem, loss of hope and creativity, self-destructive tendencies, lack of warmth and lack of energy. It is recommended to defeat suicidal tendencies and other forms of emotional distress.

Although employed primarily as an amulet for focusing the mind, citrine is also supposed to protect the wearer from a variety of bodily complaints, especially those connected with the digestive and circulatory systems.

In another capacity, citrine has been called the Merchant's Stone. There is a school of thought that believes in placing a single crystal, or a cluster of crystals, in a safe, till or cash box to magically increase financial income. As is clear from this practice, the crystals are thought to help in gaining wealth and also in keeping it.

Its reputation is not, however, without blemish and there are those who believe that it is one of the seriously unlucky stones and who avoid it at all costs.

A lucky citrine key-ring. Varying in colour from yellow to golden-brown, citrine is a form of quartz.

DIAMOND

Diamonds are not merely 'a girl's best friend'. For men, they have, since the 11th century, also been viewed as providing magical protection in battle. Being the hardest of all stones, diamonds are inevitably associated with invincibility.

I N MANY PLACES, diamonds have been considered as a useful protection (for either sex) against insanity, failure, weakness and cowardice. A diamond received as a gift is said to be more potent than one that is purchased (which is presumably another way of saying that you can't buy sanity, success, strength or courage). Diamonds can also be used to improve faith, inspiration, endurance and concentration. And, if that were not enough, they also protect the wearer from sorcery, poison, the plague, nightmares, anger, loss of friendship and being manipulated by others.

Diamond, known as the King of Crystals, is popular in engagement rings because it is said to have the power to increase love between a man and a woman. To be most effective a diamond should always be worn on the left side of the body and should be set in gold rather than some other metal.

Because diamonds are so valuable, it would seem logical to suppose that the bigger they were, the greater would be their protective power. Strangely, this is not the case. According to popular legend, very large diamonds should never be worn as amulets because they bring bad luck, and some of the largest of them are thought to carry a curse. Three of the most famous – the Regent, the Koh-i-Noor and the Hope diamonds – were owned by tragic figures who suffered every imaginable misfortune while the precious stones were in their personal possession.

The Hope Diamond has the darkest history of all. Successive owners or wearers suffered the following:

'Diamonds are a girl's best friend', sang Marilyn Monroe, although they failed her in the end.

1 financial ruin;

2 disgrace for involvement in black masses and child sacrifice;

3 mob-lynching and decapitation;

4 public execution;

5 robbery followed by death in poverty;

6 suicide;

7 death in mysterious circumstances;

8 marriage collapse followed by another death in poverty;

9 financial ruin;

10 madness leading to suicide;

11 murder by shooting;

12 murder by stabbing;

13 murder by being thrown over a precipice;

14 loss of a throne;

15 death by drowning;

16 another death from drowning, this time on the *Titanic* on the way to collect the diamond;

17 sudden death of mother, son and two servants shortly after buying it;

18 financial ruin and madness;

19 suicide of daughter.

With this amazing catalogue of calamities spanning several centuries, it is little wonder that the Hope diamond was thought to carry a curse. An alternative explanation, of course, is that those who covet great diamonds are often high-risk adventurers who court disaster.

Finally, there is a curious French tradition that says that a diamond placed under the pillow of a wife will reveal whether she has been unfaithful to her husband. How he judges this is not clear.

JET

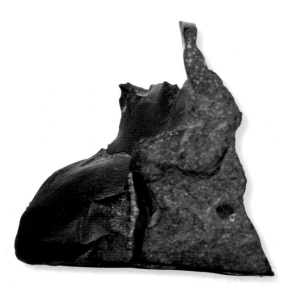

THIS STONE, A compact, dense form of coal, was known as 'Black Amber' in the Middle Ages and became immensely popular as an amulet to protect the wearer against a wide variety of diseases and ailments, against witchcraft and demons, and against melancholy and anxiety. Its effect was said to be greatest in the case of manic-depressives.

It was also thought to guard against poison, snake-bites, possession and nightmares. With its dense black colour it was thought to absorb negative influences and dispose of them.

In Italy, jet became one of the favourite materials for fashioning small amulets in the shape of gesticulating hands making the horn-sign or the fig-sign. This combination gave a double message to the powers of darkness – both the jet and the gesture sending clear signals to the Evil Eye.

The lengths to which people would go to acquire this stone, in order to manufacture magical amulets, are amazing. It has been proved that some of the jet used in ancient Mesopotamia, centuries before the birth of Christ, was mined at Whitby in northern England. It is extraordinary to think of pre-Christian traders, probably Phoenicians, carrying Yorkshire stone all the way to the Middle East to make lucky charms, and it emphasizes just how seriously such objects were treated in the days of the ancient civilizations.

It has even been suggested that the use of coal as a fuel was originally inspired by the burning of small pieces of jet in magical rituals. Jet itself was, of course, far too valuable to be used as fuel, but occasionally a small piece would be ignited to produce fumes that were thought to be effective in driving away reptiles or in dealing with 'strangulation of the womb'. The discovery that the cruder, much more common form of jet – namely coal – was being employed as a practical fuel seems to have shocked ancient travellers when they arrived in locations where there were naturally occurring rocky outcrops of the mineral. They returned home to report that, to their astonishment, the natives in these northern regions were so ignorant of the value of 'Black Amber' that they were burning it simply to keep themselves warm.

LAPIS LAZULI

THIS BEAUTIFUL MINERAL, sometimes known as the Night Stone or the Stone of Truth, has been favoured by jewellers for thousands of years. Because of its deep blue colour, it became a symbol of the heavens. In fact, its name means literally 'Stone of Heaven'.

It is considered to have all-purpose protective value, keeping its wearer safe from any kind of harm. More specifically, it defends against depression, grief and sadness. In addition, it is supposed to improve faithfulness, love and psychic sensitivity. Also, since it symbolized good vision, its intense colour being linked to the blue of the eye, it was thought to protect the wearer against eye diseases.

Sometimes referred to as the Children's Stone, lapis lazuli is supposed to protect young ones from fear and from childhood respiratory diseases, such as asthma and whooping cough. In ancient Egypt it was used to guard children from the emotional disturbances caused by incest. A more general, magical function of this mineral was to banish shyness and introversion and to assist in cases of autistic children.

In addition, lapis lazuli also has the reputation of being a fertility amulet. Yet another name for it was the Stop Stone, a reference to the fact that some women wore it as a form of protection against miscarriage and abortion.

CORNELIAN

THIS MINERAL IS known as the 'friendly stone' because its reputation covers such a wide range of healing powers. It is said to protect against many diseases and body malfunctions, loss of both physical and mental energy, lack of concentration, and anti-social feelings. In particular, it is reputed to protect the wearer from other people's envy. It also guards against vocal weaknesses and poor speech.

Cornelian's glowing yellow-orange colour has made it a favourite protective stone since the days of ancient Egypt, when it was the preferred gem for making the heart-shaped amulets that gave it its name. In the Islamic countries of the Middle East it is still one of the favourite stones for making sacred amulets which have words from the Koran engraved upon the surface. When Napoleon was in Egypt he acquired a cornelian on which was written an Arabic inscription. It is said that, because he was told it carried such impressive protective powers, he had it fixed on his watch-chain and would never be without it.

There is, incidentally, some confusion over the name of this stone. Many people today incorrectly call it the carnelian rather than the cornelian. This error began because it was thought that the word was derived from the Latin for flesh, *carne*, when in reality it refers to the Latin for heart, *cor*.

EMERALD

BECAUSE IT IS green, this crystal is said to bring rain and to 'heighten our ecological conscience'. It is also supposed to improve creativity, imagination, prosperity, memory and quick-wittedness. In particular, it is reputed to protect against infertility. An emerald suitably placed in the home is believed to keep out evil spirits.

The emerald is sometimes known as the Unconditional Love Stone. It is supposed to protect the wearer's ability to love, and is listed as the best possible gift for a lover, ensuring that they will remain loyal to the giver.

According to some authors, an emerald is also guaranteed to bring prosperity to those who wear it, but bearing in mind the immense value of a large emerald, this prediction is perhaps based more on financial reality than on occult superstition.

In earlier days, emeralds were also worn to protect people from ill-health. They were thought to be particularly effective against dysentery, eye disease, leprosy, epilepsy and poisoning. In addition, wearing one during childbirth was supposed to protect the mother from pain and a difficult delivery. For the best effect, it was to be worn around the neck so that it rested on her breast.

In some Islamic countries the power of an emerald amulet is thought to be increased by engraving a verse from the Koran on its surface. In Persia it was favoured by travellers, who would bind it to their left arm with a piece of green string. And for those travellers who feared snakes, an emerald was an invaluable gem to display to the world, because if the reptiles set eyes on it, it would dazzle and even blind them: 'Blinded like serpents when they gaze upon the emerald's virgin rays.'

The Christian Church has never been keen on green and has traditionally viewed the emerald with some suspicion, as a gem of Satan. Being the colour of springtime and fertility, and being associated with various pagan gods, one of which was called the 'prince of the emerald stone', it did not appeal to the pious early Church fathers. This disapproval has done little to damage its value, however, either as a precious stone or as a protective amulet.

JADE

GREATLY USED IN ancient times, jade is reputed to offer protection against mental weakness, many internal physical ailments, eye diseases and defects, and painful childbirth.

It is also thought to make the wearer extremely rich and in modern times has become a favourite source of amulets for gamblers, especially in the realms of horse-racing.

In China, where a good piece of jade is considered the most precious of all stones, there is a long tradition of wearing jade amulets carved into the shape of animals. Bats and storks have been the favourite models for Body Guards to protect the wearer against an early death. At weddings, jade butterflies are offered as gifts to symbolize and ensure lasting love. Part of the explanation for China's obsession with jade stems from the Oriental legend that this stone was originally formed from the solidified sperm of the great Chinese Dragon, after it had scattered its seed on the earth. Even in modern times, some Chinese businessmen will not engage in an important transaction without holding a favourite jade amulet in their hand to protect their interests.

One of the strangest features of protective jade is the way it was used in the Americas before the appearance of Columbus. The Spaniards arriving from Europe in these new lands already brought with them a widespread superstition that Jade amulets were particularly valuable in protecting against kidney problems. They were astonished to discover, not only that the indigenous peoples of the New World also carried jade amulets, but that they too wore them as a defence against kidney disease and bladder stones. This extraordinary coincidence has never been explained.

HEMATITE

JASPER

As A Body Guard, this heavy, opaque, metallic-black stone is supposed to provide protection against bodily weaknesses, stress and lack of courage. In particular, it is thought to guard against non-productive activities, dreaminess and vagueness when making decisions. It will, it is claimed, help to release you from old inhibitions and enhance your 'personal magnetism'.

When the Romans made hematite sacred to Mars, their god of war, amulets of this stone became popular with the army, especially when worn for protection in battle.

In modern times, the most remarkable claim for this particular stone amulet is that it 'helps gonorrhoea'. Quite how it does this is not explained, but it may have something to do with the theory that it 'aids the flow of yin and yang energies in the nervous system'.

Known as the Supreme Nurturer, or simply as the Talisman, because it is so popular among psychic healers, jasper is believed to protect the body from almost all kinds of ailments, especially those connected with the liver and bladder. It is said to reactivate the immune system and slow down the ageing process.

In addition, it is claimed to provide relief from snake-bites and from drought. Dowsers are said to seek its help when searching for water. More recently it has been employed during bereavement to avoid the deep depressions that sometimes follow a serious loss.

Some writers say jasper can be actively employed as a magnet to attract sexual partners. Others say that it increases self-control and caution in moments of passion. If both are correct, this could prove to be a somewhat frustrating amulet.

RUBY

ESCRIBED AS ONE of the most precious of all stones, the Stone of Nobility, with a true pigeon's-blood colour, ruby is supposed to provide protection against nothing less than unhappiness, bad fortune, quarrels, indignities, evil thoughts, enemy attacks, poison, ill-health, mental disorders, sexual excesses and early death, not to mention floods and storms.

It is also claimed to be effective against feelings of anxiety. This particular magical property is reflected in a popular Victorian verse on the subject of the birthstone for the month of July:

'The glowing ruby should adorn those who in warm July are born. Then they be exempt and free, from love's doubt and anxiety.'

In Burma, the ruby was given extra powers by being embedded in the teeth or flesh of its owner, rather than simply worn as jewellery. If directly attached to the body in this way, a ruby was thought to protect the wearer from injury in battle. In India, where this gem was called the Lord of the Precious Stones, rubies were especially associated with the protection of royalty – presumably because only they could afford to wear them.

Rubies have been credited with many protective powers, guarding against everything from poison to sexual excess.

SAPPHIRE

Pope Innocent III, who instructed his bishops to wear sapphire rings, the colour of their stones being symbolic of heaven.

A SACRED GEM OFTEN worn by kings to ward off evil, sapphire is supposed to be particularly effective at detecting treachery, resisting spells and pacifying enemies. It is also said to act as a useful Body Guard against diseases, especially those connected with the eyes.

It derives its strength, like lapis lazuli, from its blue colour, which is thought to represent the heavens. This endows it with the virtues of truth and chastity and empowers it to protect the wearer against loss of innocence. It was presumably because of this that, in the 12th century, the aptly named Pope Innocent III gave instructions that his bishops should wear sapphire rings.

According to one widespread tradition, a sapphire amulet is especially helpful in improving the state of the mind. It is said to increase clarity of thought, dispel confusion and bring relief to sufferers from nervous disorders. An anonymous Victorian verse states: 'A maiden born when autumn leaves are rustling in September's breeze, a sapphire on her brow should bind, 'twill cure diseases of the mind.'

A cloudy form of sapphire, when polished and viewed in a certain light, reveals a six-pointed star. These gems used to be called Star Stones, or Stones of Destiny, and were inevitably considered to have special powers, particularly for lovers.

AGATE

AGATE IS SAID to protect the wearer from danger, disharmony, cowardice, insomnia, nightmares, the Evil Eye and even poor metabolism – clearly a versatile mineral. It is sometimes called the Fire Stone as it is believed to be able to fire up the body and bring renewed energy to the wearer. It has also been described as the Stone of the Wanderer, because it is thought to encourage change.

One tradition sees the agate as especially important in protecting the soil. According to this, if a gardener wears an agate on his hand, his garden will flourish; and if a farmer attaches an agate to his agricultural equipment, his crops will improve. In parts of the Middle East this concept, of its ability to increase rewards from the ground, extends the powers of agate to revealing where hidden treasure is buried.

According to the ancient Romans, for its magical powers to prove effective, the agate was to be worn as a stone in a finger-ring. This idea appears to have been long-lasting, because 2,000 years later a popular Victorian verse also mentions an agate ring: 'Who comes with summer to this earth, and owes to June her date of birth, with ring of agate on her hand, can health, wealth and long life command.'

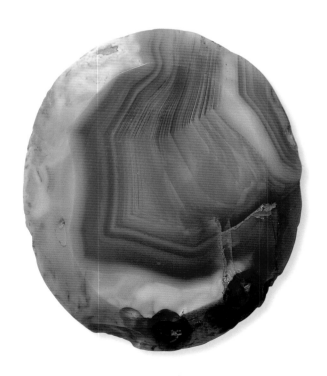

AQUAMARINE

OBSIDIAN

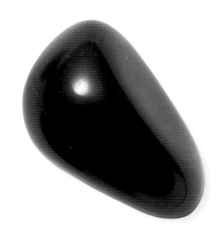

THIS PALE BLUE-green stone, looking like crystalline sea water, is known as the Serene One. It is believed to enhance mental clarity, to soothe those who wear it and to relax them, protecting them from the stresses of the day. On the modern scene, it is claimed to be the perfect amulet to keep at bay temptations involving drug abuse, its 'angelic essence' bringing a peace and mental balance that supposedly eliminates the need for artificial stimulants.

Sometimes known as the Stone of Courage, it is said to make its owners more courageous, especially in the face of death. It is also supposed to guard them from undue pessimism.

Because of its colouring, aquamarine has long been a favourite amulet for sailors at sea, protecting them, it is said, from the many dangers of the ocean. If they are fishermen, it is believed to help them obtain a good catch.

It has also been called the Stone of the Seer and Mystic because it has a delicate tone in which 'magicians can see visions'.

THIS DARK VOLCANIC glass, known as Black Velvet, is supposed to protect the wearer from indecision and from mental blocks and is also said to absorb negative energy. It has the reputation of guarding gentle people from abuse by those who are more forceful. If you take an obsidian amulet to bed with you, it is reputed to rid you of unpleasant thought-patterns while you sleep. Its devotees also claim that it alleviates viral and bacterial inflammations.

Mirrors made from obsidian have been used for divination in Central and South America for many years. And in 16th-century Europe, it was seriously believed by some authorities that angels could send messages through discs of this unusual stone.

The most popular form of this beautiful gem is 'snowflake obsidian' which has small white patches, like fallen snowflakes, scattered over its black surface. Known as the Stone of Purity, it is thought to help in removing the unwanted and unnecessary elements in life and re-creating a serene and simple balance.

MOONSTONE

A GOOD-LUCK STONE from India, where it was considered to be sacred, moonstone is said to make lovers more passionate, and is sometimes given by a hopeful groom to his bride on their wedding day. It is a favourite gem for inducing trances. Sometimes called the Mother Earth Stone, it has often been recommended for protection against women's reproductive problems, especially infertility and difficult childbirth. It has also been used as a protection against obesity and against selfishness.

In another tradition it was given the name of the Traveller's Stone because it was a favourite protective amulet for those who had to undertake a perilous journey. In earlier days, before powerful artificial light was available, it was probably hoped that carrying a moonstone would somehow assist in providing the clear, moonlit skies that would help the travellers on their way. Because of its association with the moon (which is supposed to be reflected in the sheen of the stone) it is also believed to protect sleepers from nightmares and, when awake, to help them to defend themselves against the hostile creatures that become active in the dark hours of the night.

Moonstone has given us the expression 'once in a blue moon'. In India it was believed that, once every 21 years, the sun and the moon would be in a special relationship to one another and that this would create the perfect conditions for blue moonstones to be washed up on the shore.

Perhaps the most curious claim for the moonstone amulet is that it can make the man who wears it both 'famous and invisible'. Even by occult standards this seems a little far-fetched, unless of course Lord Lucan has been wearing one.

SERPENTINE

TIGER EYE

ERPENTINE HAS BEEN used for making amulets since the days of ancient Egypt, when it was often employed in the manufacture of scarabs. Usually it is a rather opaque stone, but there is a translucent variety known as 'noble' serpentine, which is the most highly valued.

Because the surface of this stone is thought to resemble the skin of a snake, its use as an amulet has been primarily to protect against snake-bites, insect stings and other forms of poisoning.

In addition to protecting against poisons, serpentine has also enjoyed a secondary role as a cure for rheumatism, with pieces of it strapped to the parts of the body most affected. It was also reputed to be able to draw out the liquid from watery blisters, if applied to their surfaces.

NOTHER FORM OF quartz, tiger eye is said to protect against digestive ailments, cowardice, poor perception and lack of insight. In earlier days it was considered to be a valuable protection against the Evil Eye.

Tiger eye has sometimes been called the Stone of Independence. This has given it a mixed reputation, since it is supposed to make the wearers less reliant on others and more dependent on themselves. In one direction, this builds character, but in the other it breaks up partnerships and is then supposed to encourage divorce.

Among Arabs a completely different tradition exists. There, if a husband is about to undertake a long journey, he gives his wife a drink of milk in which he has dipped his tiger-eye amulet. If, after he has done this, she is unfaithful to him in his absence, it is believed that she will not become pregnant by her lover. This is a strange example of a contraceptive amulet and it is difficult to see how such a superstition could have arisen, unless of course it is an example of a husband symbolically keeping his (tiger) eye on his wife.

TOPAZ

KNOWN AS THE Abundant One, this is a mineral so powerful that it was believed to be capable of curing both blindness and the plague. Topaz, encountered in many different colours, was also said to protect the wearer from ill-health, cowardice and loss of integrity. In the Middle Ages it was worn on the left arm, set in a gold bracelet, to guard against the Evil Eye.

Also called the Gem of Love, topaz is said to protect the wearer from any cooling in a relationship. According to a Victorian verse: 'Who first comes to this world below, with drear November's fog and snow, should prize the Topaz' amber hue, emblem of friends and lovers true.'

This was the favoured stone of the Roman Emperor Hadrian. He always wore a talismanic ring in which was set a topaz inscribed with a Latin phrase stating that the Almighty would overrule nature. Roman authors gave this stone yet another title, the Stone of Strength, because they felt that it would protect them from dangers and evils when travelling.

The emperor Hadrian, whose favourite amulet was an inscribed, talismanic topaz.

GARNET

KNOWN AS THE Day-dreamer, this crystal is reputed to protect the wearer against physical weakness and to defend against loss of compassion. As with many other amuletic gems, this stone is also said to protect against ill-health, poison and depression.

It is known, too, as the Stone of Compassion. As a provider of loyalty and constancy, garnet is celebrated in this popular Victorian verse about the birthstone for the month of January: 'By her who is this month born, no gems save garnet should be worn; they will ensure her constancy, true friendship and fidelity.'

In addition, it has sometimes been referred to as the Passion Stone because it is supposed to increase sexual energy and sensitivity and to protect against any lack of sexual

balance. Worn as an amulet (especially a heart-shaped one), it is believed to help attract a loving partner. Placed under the pillow at night, it wards off bad dreams and evil nocturnal spirits. As if that were not enough, it also guards against being struck by lightning.

Finally, it has been seen as a magical aid to women, especially in connection with problems of bleeding and the womb. The name garnet comes from the Latin *granatum*, meaning pomegranate (itself a symbol of fertility and the womb).

In Italy it was also known as the Stone of Widowhood because widows favoured necklaces made of garnet-beads.

For this 17th-century Italian widow, the garnet protected against depression.

79

TURQUOISE

ONYX

ALTHOUGH THIS PARTICULAR gem was highly esteemed in the ancient world, for some reason it fell into disrepute in the Middle Ages. Then, anyone wearing it was said to be 'exposed to the assault of demons' and subjected to ugly visions at night. It was also supposed to cause arguments between friends and involvement in lawsuits, and generally to 'depress the mind'. As a result, it was occasionally referred to as the Stone of Separation.

In modern times it appears to have regained its earlier, good reputation and is described as a gem to protect against lack of clarity of sight and mind. It also supposedly aids concentration, banishes grief, protects against unwise decision-making and assists with self-discipline and sexual self-control. It has often been pressed into service against the Evil Eye.

TURQUOISE, THE TURKISH Stone or Lucky Stone, is the most popular of all amulet stones and has been credited with a wide variety of protective properties. In addition to being effective against poison and ill-health, it is said to guard its owner against failure, poverty and lack of success in the hunt. Its association with success is emphasized by this anonymous Victorian verse: 'If cold December gave you birth, the month of snow and ice and mirth, place on your hand a turquoise blue, success will bless whate'er you do.'

In earlier centuries it was also employed as a horse-amulet to protect the animals from harm. In Turkey turquoise was known as the Horseman's Talisman. It was believed there that any rider who carried one would never suffer any injury if he fell from his horse.

To the ancient Aztecs it was the Stone of the Gods. They sometimes tied turquoise amulets to their weapons to improve their effectiveness in attack.

A cautionary note

The foregoing gemstones are the favourite 'magic rocks'. It should be pointed out that the protective properties listed for each one have been drawn from several authorities and that these authorities do not always

agree. Some minerals do have a reputation for protecting most effectively against one particular form of harm, but much wider powers have been ascribed to most of them. Some of the powers are so wide that the mineral in question can be considered as virtually all-protective.

Of the 27 gems listed here, 8 are now being widely marketed as inexpensive 'lucky-charm' pendants. These are amethyst, clear quartz, citrine, hematite, malachite, rose quartz, tiger eye and turquoise. They are offered for sale on the Internet and at New Age shops.

Although these crystal amulets are increasingly popular as lucky charms, meditation devices or healing stones, it has to be said that, if the claims made

More and more crystals, like this beautiful 'orange phantom' quartz, are being used in healing rituals, but scientists remain highly sceptical about their value.

for them were all valid, a simple necklace or a pendant, comprising one of each of them, or a pocketful or purseful of them, should provide such massive protection for their owner that he or she would never have a moment's physical illness or emotional disturbance, ever again. Unfortunately life is not like that. We all suffer from physical or mental problems from time to time. If solving them was as easy as carrying a small, inexpensive crystal, the entire human population would be doing it. The fact that they are not speaks for itself.

New Age shops today are full of crystals of many different kinds and even though their healing powers are unproven, their beauty is undeniable.

THE METALS

THERE IS NO SCIENTIFIC validity in any of the many claims for the magical influences of metals. What is surprising about the myths attached to them is that they have managed to survive at all in modern times. And yet there are sincere individuals today who are intent on turning their backs on new scientific knowledge and insist instead on returning to the primitive mystical practices of the alchemists.

Recognizing that few enthusiasts would be sufficiently eccentric to accept a full return to medieval alchemy, the new, 'practical alchemists' suggest that alchemy must be thought of in a 'broader sense, as the art of magical transformation through working with crystals, gems and mineral ores from the

The Little Gold Man of Scandinavia – a modern replica of an ancient amulet – gold to attract gold.

Earth'. This, they claim, will put it on a new footing and will make it more easily acceptable.

The methods used are not those of the medieval laboratory chemist, trying to turn base metals into gold, but much more simple procedures such as the 'laying on' of various minerals – metals, stones, crystals or gems – or by holding them in the hand, while concentrating on thoughts of spiritual renewal. The main focus of attention today is on the various forms of crystal. These are used in what is termed 'crystal healing' or 'crystal medicine' and are also worn as crystal amulets, in the form of pendants, rings, bracelets, anklets, necklaces, headgear or brooches.

Gold

In the language of magic, gold possesses a potent healing energy. It 'extends awareness', 'excites the masculine aspect of human nature', and 'motivates the patient to wellness'. To the magician, these are the reasons why it has been used as the basis for so many Body Guards over the centuries. To the scientist, it is the fact that gold does not tarnish and never loses its intense golden glow that gives it a powerful appeal.

In Scandinavia, a small gift of gold used to be placed in every new house to protect its owners from misfortune, the principle being that 'gold attracts gold'. It was the custom for a young couple to be given a gold amulet on their wedding day, to incorporate in their first house. The message of the amulet was: 'I am calling to the Gold to come to my house and family and bring me fortune and wealth.' The offering took the form of a tiny, thin 'Little Gold Man' of a characteristic design. It was less than 10mm (⅜in) in length and was traditionally placed in one of the post-holes of the main supports of the house. This home-protecting ritual began in AD 400 and examples have been discovered by

archaeologists in Norway, Sweden and Denmark. Today it is possible to obtain modern, gold replicas of the stylized 'Little Gold Man' that can be worn as lucky charms.

Silver

In contrast to gold's affinity to the masculine, silver is seen as essentially feminine in character. If gold is the metal of the sun, silver is the metal of the moon. The healing quality of silver is said to be that of enhancing receptivity and intuition, and of increasing psychic awareness. It is believed to bring a soothing quietness to the personality.

It is said that if a woman wants to make a wish she should do so while turning a silver coin in her hand and looking at the moon.

Mercury

This dangerous substance was believed to release the hidden depths of personality and to increase longevity. It is hard to see how this myth could have arisen, as mercury could, in reality, only do harm.

Copper

Copper is claimed to be able to enhance clear mental images and to increase feelings of love, harmony and peace. It is thought to be one of the best transmitters of healing energy and is therefore often employed in the manufacture of magical instruments.

In mystical terms, just as gold was linked with the sun and silver with the moon, so copper became associated with the planet Venus. This was because the main source of ancient copper was the island of Cyprus, officially the Sacred Isle of the goddess Venus. It was through this connection that copper became endowed with its magical properties.

Iron

Iron, for no immediately obvious reason, is said to excite and increase reproductive energies. Also, in some cultures, it is strongly believed that iron will offer protection from demons and other evil forces. Instead of 'touching wood' for good luck, they 'touch iron'.

Tin

Despite its dull colour, tin is felt to provide prosperity and growth and to increase emotional and spiritual qualities. It is said to protect an individual from arrogance, feelings of unjustified superiority, thoughtlessness and lack of reasoning ability. Used in the house and garden, it is, rather curiously, recommended for keeping insects at bay.

Lead

Lead, despite the serious risks of lead-poisoning, has been viewed as a metal that can help to focus thoughts, stabilize the mind, and protect against both physical and mental weakness. It is also reputed, rather strangely, to guard against failure in pursuits involving music, sport and business management.

HORSE-BRASSES

A draught-horse on display at a country fair, decorated with ornate trappings and richly festooned with glistening horse-brasses, is a magnificent sight. In modern times we look upon such displays as being purely decorative, but there is much more to them than that. As equine accessories, horse-brasses may today be little more than appealing collectors' items, but in origin they are important, magical Body Guards dating back to pagan times.

For thousands of years the horse was the key to human mobility, and this made it a precious possession that deserved all the protection it could be given. Because it was such an impressive, indispensable animal, superstitious minds were convinced that it would be especially appealing to the forces of darkness. And it was argued that, although the evil spirits would use every opportunity to attack and incapacitate the horse, they would, in particular, focus their assaults on those animals that were being paraded on important celebratory occasions. If there was a great procession, a spectacular ceremony or a festive gathering where horses were on show, that was where the Evil Eye would be most likely to cast its withering glance, causing injury, sickness and disease wherever its gaze came to rest.

Centuries ago it was decided to protect the ceremonial horse from the Evil Eye by equipping it with images of the pagan gods – images which, with their supernatural powers, would repel the evil spirits and send them scurrying back into the dark world from which they had emerged. The images used included suns, crescent moons, hearts and lotus-flowers, evoking the sun-god, the moon-goddess and the gods of ancient Egypt. Other ancient symbols employed were the swastika, in its role representing the sun moving through the heavens, sacred hands, stars, wheels and horns. In addition to their sacred impact, these adornments had one special quality – they glistened and shone, flashing golden as the horse moved in the sunlight. This gave them the added advantage of being able to reflect the Evil Eye and they were kept highly polished to improve this ability.

The simple idea was that, if the Evil One looked up at the horse it would see its own eye reflected in the polished brass surfaces and in this way would defeat itself. The most important of all the early horse-brasses was therefore the 'sunflash', a plain, circular disc that acted like a little mirror. This was usually given pride of place on the centre of the horse's forehead, but it was also sometimes suspended in such a way that it swung back and forth as the horse moved. These 'swingers' had the added advantage that they were thought to dazzle the Evil Eye.

In Victorian times the protective value of these adornments became less important. People became less superstitious and more concerned with displaying their status and wealth. This resulted in a dramatic increase in the number and variety of harness ornaments, with literally hundreds of new designs being introduced. None of these new designs had the slightest protective significance. They were purely decorative. In the 20th century this submerging of the protective by the decorative continued, year by year, until the original significance of the brasses was almost forgotten.

In addition to brasses, some horse-harnesses display small bells that swing back and forth as the animal moves. The incessant tinkling sound created by these bells was thought to be another way of frightening away harmful spirits, giving the horse a second line of defence against the supernatural.

THE ARROWHEAD

A carved stone arrowhead has occasionally been employed as an amulet, but has never played a major protective role. This is probably because genuine ones are difficult to obtain, and cheap copies would not be considered effective.

CARRIED AS an amulet, a neolithic flint arrowhead is said to guard its owner from enemies, jealousy, illness, misfortune and all kinds of evil spirits. Placed in a car or hung over the front door of a house, it is also recommended as a deterrent to thieves and burglars.

It is also claimed that arrowheads are valuable 'love charms' and that to wear one ensures that the person you love will respond to your advances. In this role, it is clear that the arrowhead amulet is being seen as a token of Cupid's arrow, which symbolically pierces the heart of the loved one.

The use of arrowhead amulets goes back many centuries. Writing 2,000 years ago, Pliny mentions the gruesome tradition that if an arrowhead is to be really effective as a love charm it must first be obtained in a special way – by digging it out of a body into which an arrow has been shot.

In the Middle Ages, arrowhead amulets were thought to have powerful magical properties because it was believed that they had been manufactured by fairies. They were called Elf-shots and were worn as pendants to repel the Evil Eye. Their association with the fairies resulted from the way they were discovered. After heavy rain had washed away topsoil in the countryside, it sometimes exposed ancient arrowheads in fields or lanes, where they had previously remained concealed for hundreds of years. Because these strange little pieces of carved stone suddenly appeared, as if by magic, it was assumed by superstitious rural people that they must have been left there by fairy workmen. (In Japan, an alternative explanation was given: there it was claimed that they had been accidentally dropped by flying spirits.)

An arrowhead amulet was also favoured in medieval attempts to cure diseases. To achieve this it had to be dipped in water. The liquid was then thought to possess special curative properties. In other words, the arrowhead 'blessed' the water and endowed it with magical properties. This was presumably because the amulet enlisted the aid of the 'good fairies' who would defeat the powers of darkness causing the disease.

Because, in earlier times, arrows were in use all over the globe, it is not surprising that many different cultures have developed their own interpretation of the value of arrowhead amulets. To give just a few examples, they were used in Italy to protect from the Evil Eye; in Arabia to protect the blood; in Ireland to protect the Elves; in Malaya to bring good luck; in what is now New Mexico among the Acoma to protect their children; among the Zuni to keep their women safe when travelling at night; in France to encourage an early childbirth; and so on, with different uses around the world.

Arrowheads were often so highly valued that they were mounted in gold.

Arrowhead amulets have been worn for thousands of years and are still on sale in many countries today.

THE BEZOAR STONE

In earlier days, when the nobility went in fear of poisoning, it was the custom to drop a Bezoar Stone into a glass of wine or water as a magical protection. The stone was thought to be able to detect and even neutralize any poison that was present. This precaution was widely practised until the 18th century, when scientific knowledge began to discredit a large number of common superstitious practices.

AT THE BEGINNING of the 18th century, in *Bailey's Dictionary* of 1730, Bezoar is still defined as 'a medicinal stone brought from both the East and West Indies, accounted a sovereign counter-poison and an excellent cheerer of the heart'. This definition was soon to change however. By 1788, Bezoar Stones were described in *Howard's Cyclopedia* as 'stony concre-

The gut contents of slaughtered goats have always been a favoured source of magical Bezoars.

tions formed in…the stomachs of goats, harts, horses, asses, cows, etc…by the credulity of former times celebrated as…a subduer of poisons'. Interestingly, the author goes on to say: 'There are two forms of bezoar kept in the shops…oriental and occidental…' In other words, learned men were now laughing at the magical powers ascribed to the Bezoar Stones, but despite this enlightened attitude there was still a thriving trade in them. Indeed, they were so popular that many fakes were made, including three sent to Napoleon by the King of Persia. Weight for weight, genuine ones were more valuable than gold.

In addition to being placed in suspect drinks, they were also sometimes powdered and swallowed, or 'worn around the neck, as preservatives'. In other words, they were employed, not only as magical objects, but also as medicines and as protective amulets. But what, precisely, were they?

There appears to have been some confusion about their true origin. One of the earliest reports romantically pictured them as the solidified tears of a deer that had wept with pain after being bitten by a venomous snake. Later, more scientific works described them in pedestrian terms as 'concretions found in the fourth stomach of many ruminants, notably the bezoar goat'. In other words, they were objects similar to hairballs or gallstones, small lumps of foreign matter hardened and enlarged by calcium deposits forming around them. They must first have been discovered when game animals were being butchered, and, because of their oddity – they were often spheroid, smooth and glossy – rapidly acquired mystical powers.

There is, however, another, completely different source. Some Bezoars were made of solid stone and had a slightly elongated, segmented shape. These were found, not inside game animals but embedded in the surface of rocks. Because of their strange shape they were assumed to have the same magical properties as the other Bezoar Stones. They were, in fact, small fossils of a special kind, being the petrified remains of prehistoric animal droppings. Their true nature was discovered by the English Victorian geologist William Buckland, who gave them the new, scientific name of coprolites (meaning dung-stones).

As with many other forms of protective object, the appeal of the famous Bezoar Stones was not entirely lost in the modern, scientific age. As recently as 1879 – long after they had been discredited as poison neutralizers – one was offered for sale in Texas and realized the then enormous price of $250. Even as late as 1933 a Tennessee newspaper was running a classified advertisement offering one for sale. And in modern China, where alternative medical practices still abound, both horse Bezoar Stones and cow Bezoar Stones are still sold to those who wish to 'clear away toxic substances'.

BEADS

Today we take beads for granted. One of the minor forms of body decoration, a string of cheap beads is of little importance. This may be true of modern times, but it has not always been so. In earlier days, beads were often given great significance and carried powerful protective qualities.

IT HAS BEEN suggested that the role of the bead as a Body Guard can be traced back to prehistoric times when stones and pebbles with a naturally occurring hole through the centre were thought to possess special properties. Even today there are parts of the world where a pebble with a hole in it, discovered on the seashore, is believed to bring good luck. Taken home and hung over the bed, it will ensure a sound night's sleep and protect the sleeper from nightmares.

Hung up in a stable, the pebble will protect a horse from being 'hagridden'. In Victorian stables, which were often cramped and unhealthy, horses were sometimes found exhausted in the morning and the superstition developed that hags, or witches, had stolen them in the night and ridden them nearly to death. The truth was that it was the often wretched conditions of the stables that were to blame, but the stablemen could never accept that. Instead they employed anti-witch amulets, like the pierced stone, to defeat the imagined enemies of the unhappy animals. (Unfortunately these stones never seemed to be effective at protecting the poor horses from the stupidity of the stablemen themselves.)

From pierced stones it is easy to see how the concept of beads could have developed. Many of the earliest examples of beads are large and crudely shaped. Then, as technology improved, they became smaller and more perfectly fashioned. In the process, decorative considerations began to overshadow the older, protective functions. Increasingly beautiful beads became just that, objects to appeal to the eye rather than to the superstitious mind.

Only in a few instances did the old role for beads survive. Where the substance used to make them – red coral, for instance – had a strongly protective flavour, their original function sometimes managed to survive. In several parts of the world, especially around the shores of the Mediterranean, red-coral necklaces remained a popular way of protecting infants from the Evil Eye. And when it came to choosing a way to 'count one's prayers', strings of beads were the obvious choice.

'Telling the beads' of the rosary remains today as a surviving example of what can only be described as primeval 'bead magic'. As so often happens with amulets, true origins are easily forgotten.

A string of beads from ancient Egypt. Beads like these have been worn for thousands of years.

THE BIOELECTRICAL SHIELD

In 1998 the British Prime Minister's wife, Cherie Blair, was photographed wearing a 'stress-busting', metal-encased crystal amulet. The pendant was said to contain 'a magical configuration of quartz and other crystals which deflect electromagnetic radiation from modern office equipment'.

INVENTED BY A chiropractor called Dr Charles Brown in the early 1990s, the Shield has proved immensely popular, despite selling at remarkably high prices. About 22,000 of them were sold during the first eight years of manufacture by the Bioelectrical Shield Company in America. The secret formula for the pendant came to Dr Brown in a series of visions when he was lying in bed in his Montana log cabin. He heard voices inside his head telling him the special combination of minerals, the configuration and the shape that he should use. He is quoted as saying: 'The shield puts a cocoon around you. At the edge of the cocoon is a layer that spins. That spinning layer is like a gate-keeper.' Its power is said to be so strong that the locket's vortex of energy can 'deflect the stress from loved ones' and even 'blunt the rays from mobile phones'. According to the instructions, the only care needed with the device is ensuring that it is exposed to the sun's rays for a day at least once a month, to recharge the crystals inside it.

Charles Brown's wife, a therapist, believes that the Shield is especially useful to protect people from office equipment. She is quoted as saying:

Most of us are not aware of what is happening in our bodies. Electromagnetic radiation from computers has a physically measurable effect. Human beings have an energy field with a speed of 8–10 cycles per second. So if you are sitting in front of a computer you are in a head-on collision with something coming at you 45 times faster than your energy field and likely to be right in your face and your heart…Any energy that comes towards the person wearing the shield that is not compatible with them will be diverted.

Cherie Blair would seem to agree with this. In August 1998, when she mislaid her Shield, she was reported as being distressed because, she explained: 'It keeps away bad vibrations from my computer.'

The medical profession is dismissive of all these claims. A Surrey University 'quack-busters hotline' accepts that the usual placebo effect could be operating, but stresses that use of the Shield 'may do someone harm if they believe they are protected from something when they are not'.

What is unique about this amulet is that, unlike all the others in this book, it is a modern invention of the 1990s.

New technologies give rise to new superstitions. Fears that hostile forces may emanate from computers have led to a new generation of Body Guards.

Plant Power
BOTANICAL BODY GUARDS

Because of their potential healing power and their natural beauty, many kinds of flowers, fruits and plants have been used as Body Guards, all around the world. Some of these are worn in their natural state. This helps to retain their original 'green power', but it usually means that they are short-lived and have to be discarded and replaced at regular intervals. A more permanent alternative has been created by copying the shape of the plant, leaf or flower in some material such as silver or gold. And an ingenious new method sees the real botanical specimen carefully coated in some kind of permanent metal, giving the wearer the best of both worlds.

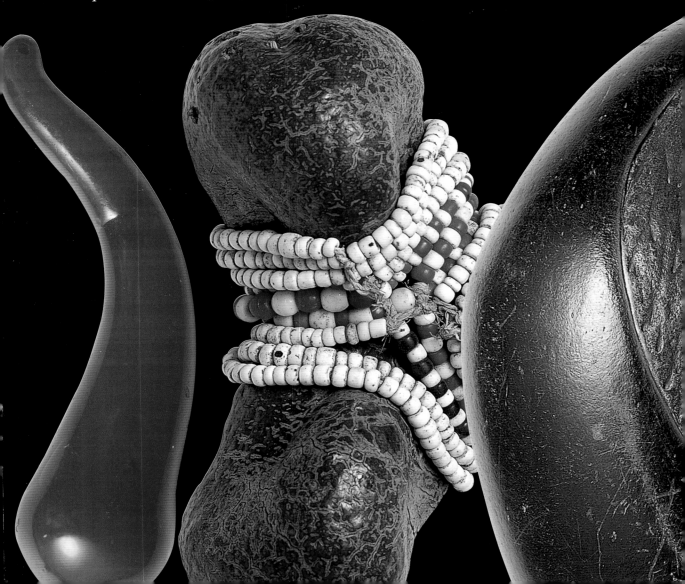

GARLIC

Garlic is well known from horror films as the peasants' defence against vampires. When threatened, the frightened villagers hang strings of garlic in their cottages, with the firm conviction that this will repel the bloodsuckers and prevent them from entering the buildings. If the threat is severe, at night they will even sleep in a necklace of garlic.

THIS POPULAR IMAGE of protective garlic is only part of a long folklore tradition associated with it, which stretches back at least 2,000 years and ranges from Europe, through the Middle East and Asia to the Orient. Roman soldiers used it to give them courage. In the Middle Ages it was carried into battle as a defence against injury. Sailors took garlic with them on sea voyages to protect themselves against shipwreck. Mountaineers wore it to protect themselves against storms and the perils of bad weather. Miners in Germany took garlic down into the mines with them, to keep at bay evil forces that could cause tunnel collapse. Bullfighters in Bolivia took a clove of garlic into the ring with them, in the hope of deflecting the bull's horns. At weddings, a bride would often carry a clove of garlic hidden in her clothes to protect her from evil.

Garlic was placed under the pillow of a sleeping baby to keep it safe at night. This was considered especially important during the period between birth and baptism, when the baby was lacking the sacred protection of the holy water.

These are only a few of the superstitions linked to this plant, some of which still survive to this day. At various times it was also worn, or hung in the home, to offer a defence against monsters, thieves, robbers, envious visitors and the blows of one's enemies. It was also believed to be an effective amulet against a staggeringly wide range of medical misfortunes, including worms, fevers, toothache, poisons, sunstroke, dropsy, hysteria, rabies, bedwetting, smallpox and even leprosy. Sometimes the protection required special procedures. To prevent hepatitis, for instance, a string of 13 garlic cloves had to be worn on a cord hung around the neck for 13 days. To guard children against whooping cough, the cloves had to be placed inside their socks. Adding garlic to food was also thought to be a way of providing special protection to those who ate it. The Berbers, for example, ground up garlic and baked it in bread as a defence against infection.

Peasants collecting garlic in the 14th century. This pungent plant has been used against the forces of evil for many centuries.

The origin of the protective role of this bulbous, onion-like plant is not immediately obvious. It may have been kept alive by astute garlic salesmen, but it is doubtful if they can claim credit for the early development of its vast folklore. There is an ancient legend which states that garlic first sprang to life in the imprint of the Devil's foot as he was being driven out of paradise. This might provide it with impressive supernatural credentials, but a more down-to-earth explanation suggests that it is simply the strong-smelling breath of those who have just eaten garlic that gives it its protective power. In this view, it is considered to be so repellent that it is even capable of driving away the forces of darkness and all the miseries and diseases to which they subject the human race. Supporting this idea is the fact that the other famously pungent plant, the onion, has also been endowed with protective powers, although on a lesser scale than the garlic.

BASIL

BASIL IS AN INDIAN plant, sacred to the gods Vishnu and Krishna. When it first arrived in England, centuries ago, it was not eaten but was instead employed to 'comfort the brain' by its presence. It was also believed to protect its owner from pain, especially in the case of a woman in labour. If she clasped a root of basil in her hand during childbirth 'she shall be delivered without pain'. Its name is thought to have come from the idea that it could be used against the Evil Eye of the dreaded basilisk, a terrifying monster that could kill with its stare.

A pot of basil displayed on a special stone bracket on the front wall of an old Maltese house.

On the island of Malta the magical, protective properties of basil led to a strange ritual. If there was a virgin in the house she needed extra protection and basil was employed to ensure this. The link between virgins and basil meant that, if a particular family wished to advertise the presence in their home of a young girl ready to be married, all they had to do was to put their virgin-guarding basil on the outside of the house. To this end, small stone brackets were built onto all the old Maltese houses, near an upstairs window.

This basil display was necessary, because, in earlier centuries, a young woman was seldom allowed to venture outside her house. It was said – perhaps with slight exaggeration – that she would only appear in public twice in her life, once to be married and once to be buried. Apart from those special occasions she was a recluse, living out her life behind high walls that protected her from all the dangers of the outside world. So, for her, the basil display announcing her availability was essential.

THE BAY TREE

THE MEDITERRANEAN SHRUB known as the bay laurel or bay tree has a long and complex history in its role as a Body Guard, dating from the time of ancient Greece.

It is a common practice today to place a small bay tree on either side of a front door, so that anyone entering the building must pass between them. As with so many of our modern fashions, what is now considered to be purely decorative was at one time magical and protective. The bay tree was once thought to be especially effective in guarding the home from harm. A 16th-century author, Thomas Lupton, wrote that 'neither falling sickness, neither devil, will infest or hurt one in that place where a bay-tree is'. And Shakespeare, in *Richard II*, assumed his audience would immediately understand that if there was a major disaster it could only mean that the bay trees had failed in their magical duty:

Tis thought the king is dead: we will not stay.
The bay trees in our country are all withered.

In ancient Greece the bay laurel was sacred to Apollo and became a symbol of victory and honour. As a result, victory wreaths were fashioned from laurel leaves. Since Apollo killed the Cyclops (who made thunderbolts), the bay could not be struck by lightning and was therefore also adopted as a shield against thunderstorms. So bay trees placed outside the door of a house were, in effect, acting as lightning conductors.

In time, this protection spread to include all kinds of bad weather and eventually was extended to become a blanket defence against witchcraft.

Two bay trees on either side of a front door, protecting the house from evil spirits.

CHILLI

The red chilli pepper may at first sight seem like an unusual choice for an amulet to protect against the Evil Eye, but its use in this role has been extremely common in Italy. The explanation has nothing to do with the fact that the chilli is hot in taste. It is the shape and colour that are important, because they make the chilli look like a small animal horn.

A N ANIMAL-HORN pendant has been popular in Italy for centuries. Called the Corno, it was worn in gold, silver, red coral or the original, natural horn. The red-coral version was especially popular and it was this that came to mind when Italians first saw the red chilli peppers that were imported from South America. These new peppers soon became favourites in the kitchen, but because they looked so much like the red-coral horn amulets, some of them were hung up in the kitchen as charms. From there they spread to the rest of the house and eventually into shops, becoming more and more popular as a cheap and easily obtained defence against the Evil Eye.

Apart from their general use against the Evil Eye, red chilli peppers were in particular employed to provide protection from the infidelity of a loved one. If a marriage partner was thought to be straying, the suspicious person placed two large dried chilli peppers under his or her own pillow, which would keep the partner faithful. Added magical power was given to the chillies if they were tied together with a red ribbon, in the form of a cross. Chilli peppers have also been used to protect a person who has been cursed. In this case, they are not worn on the body but are scattered about the house.

In recent times, the natural chilli has been replaced by an artificial one made from red plastic. During the process a strange transformation has taken place. The chilli has become slightly more horn-like. The curving shape and colour remain those of a chilli, but the smooth hardness of the amulet is the property of a horn. In other words, it is a hybrid object, half-chilli and half-horn, absorbing the amuletic power of both its natural 'parents'. Being more durable than a real chilli and (in an urban world) more easily obtained than a real horn, it has a double advantage.

This plastic chilli-horn is called upon in many ways. People who no longer fear the Evil Eye use it simply as a good-luck charm. Gamblers rub it before placing a bet, rolling dice or drawing a card.

Red chillies themselves are sometimes used as inexpensive protective charms in Italy.

Cooks keep one in the kitchen to ensure success in the preparation of meals. Drivers hang them up in their cars to protect themselves from traffic-jams, accidents and bad weather conditions. Even serious businessmen sometimes call on their aid to assist in important financial negotiations.

Once the cheap plastic chilli-horn had established itself as *the* amulet for many Italians, a demand grew for more sophisticated forms. An up-market version in gold or silver started to appear, for use as an elegant pendant. Usually more slender in shape than the plastic one, this elegant amulet caused confusion, sometimes being called a 'pepper', but more often being described as a Corno. However, a brief glance at its highly characteristic, curved shape confirms that it too is, in fact, a hybrid chilli-horn.

According to one authority, the strength of this hybrid amulet lies in the fact that, not only does it embody both parent amulets, but it also has the advantage of being a new, slightly abstracted image in its own right. It has a modern life of its own, remote from the crudely 'folksy' images of real animal horns or vegetable pods. This has somehow added to its mystique and made it popular on both sides of the Atlantic, among Italian–Americans as well as among native Italians.

HAWTHORN

THIS BUSH, ORIGINALLY known as hag-thorn, was used as a source of amulets because it was believed that witches transformed themselves into hawthorn trees. Presumably on the principle that 'it takes a witch to catch a witch', small pieces of hawthorn were placed on the outside of a house, especially on doors or windows, to protect the building and its occupants from evil spirits. It was believed that a witch attempting to enter the house would become caught up on the sharp points and torn to pieces as she struggled to break free. (It was, however, thought to be unlucky to carry the hawthorn inside the house.)

In ancient Rome there were different traditions, sprigs of hawthorn being placed near cradles to protect the sleeping infants. In some regions of Italy this practice is still followed today. Women often wore or carried hawthorn to increase their fertility, and it was sometimes employed as a protective plant for newly married couples. Some Greek brides, even today, still wear a hawthorn wreath at their weddings.

In rural districts of France, during the Easter celebrations, devout Christians may wear a sprig of spiky hawthorn in their hats as a symbolic reminder of the crown of thorns worn by Christ at His crucifixion. Some believe that the crown of thorns was actually made of hawthorn and that the red berries it produces each year are an echo of the blood shed by Christ as the sharp thorns dug into his head.

Additional magical roles for hawthorn include protection against lightning, haunting by ghosts and damage to a house by storms. In some districts, hawthorn is carried in sachets and used by fishermen to protect them from a poor catch.

HENNA

I N   A   N U M B E R   O F countries, from North Africa through the Middle East to parts of Asia, a special skin decoration is applied to a bride a few days before her wedding night. The substance used is a red-orange stain called henna, meticulously painted in delicate and elaborate patterns.

Henna cosmetics are made from the powdered leaves of a small shrub called *Lawsonia*. After a ritual bathing, the bride-to-be is dressed in her wedding finery and made to sit very still with her eyes shut while a female artist called a 'hennaria' paints the designs on her hands and feet. Once she has finished, she bandages the bride's hands and places them inside two embroidered bags to ensure that they dry without smudging. The feet may also be wrapped in pieces of linen. Usually the hands and feet stay bound up like this for a whole night. After they are exposed, the patterns will normally survive for about three to four weeks, after which they may be renewed.

Today henna painting is often purely decorative, but its true function is to provide magical protection.

The night on which this decoration takes place, with the bride surrounded by her female friends, is referred to as 'the henna night', and it has been suggested that the British term 'hen night', which was first used in the 1880s, was borrowed from this.

The designs employed – which include such motifs as stars and crosses – are thought to protect the bride from evil spirits. There is an ancient superstition that the serene happiness of the wedding ceremony will attract evil forces to the blissful couple and that they will therefore require an extra dose of protective magic. Covering the body in intricate, protective signs is seen as the best way of repelling the Evil Eye. Henna is said to possess a kind of 'virtue' which purifies the wearers from 'earthly taint' and renders them immune from the attacks of the Devil and his agents.

POMANDER

In the Middle Ages the stench of city streets was so appalling that suffering citizens felt the need for protection from the 'bad air' which they believed was causing many diseases. Their answer was to wear a small amulet called a pomander (ie 'apple of amber'). This consisted of a perforated scent-holder containing aromatic spices and herbs. It was thought that the scent emanating from them would guard the wearers from many ailments.

WHEN THE Black Death swept the land, it was claimed that even this could be held at bay by the pomander's pungent contents. The fact that many people who wore them died of the plague did not seem to deter others from continuing the tradition. One reason for the persistence of their popularity was that, in addition to their magical medical role, they also happened to create a pleasant fragrance that went some way to masking the bad street odours.

A secondary explanation was their strong link with another custom that had preceded them. For thousands of years and in most of the major religions of the world, there had been a ritual procedure in which special resins were burned as part of sacred ceremonies. These resins were placed in small perforated containers with hot coals, and the result was a pungent smoke that rose up into the air.

These smoking resin-containers were called censers or incense-burners, and they became a vital part of many church services. Unfortunately, because of the heat involved, they could only be carried while held away from the body. They could never be worn as true amulets. This problem was solved by the invention of the pomander. This could be worn as a pendant on a chain around the neck, or even on a finger as a large, cage-like ring. Fire was replaced by pungency.

Censers provided a tradition involving a perforated ball or box containing a magical substance that gave off protective fumes. The pomander was simply an easy-to-handle, second-generation version of this tradition. Both the incense-burner and the pomander emitted 'sacred vapours'.

In Scandinavia, miniature pomanders – tiny silver spheres – have often been used as token amulets. In the far north, these are worn by brides as part of their wedding costume, and also placed

A miniature German version of the protective pomander/censer.

on the sides of the cots and cradles of babies. The holes on the sphere (apertures which, with the pomander's reduced size, would be virtually invisible) have been replaced by a symbolic equivalent – tiny silver rings that hang conspicuously below it.

In recent times there has been a resurgence of interest in the wearing of pomanders and, despite the vast body of modern medical knowledge, the old superstitions have re-emerged in no uncertain terms. One company, marketing a whole range of modern pomanders, makes the impressive claim that they work 'their invisible magick directly on the electromagnetic field of the Auric body, affording protection while promoting inner and outer harmony'.

These modern pomanders are said to aid in treating many unpleasant conditions, from bronchitis, hormonal imbalance, migraines and tinnitus to nervous depression, nightmares and bedwetting. They come in different colours, each with its own protective promises. These claims are thrown into doubt, however, by the accompanying, official 'product disclaimer' which states that 'the company does not claim that its products will diagnose, heal or prevent an illness or disease'.

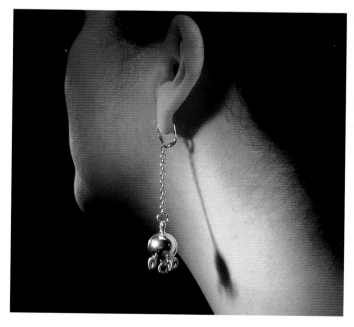

THE TRIPLE NUT

IN THE MORE remote corners of Kenya today, it is possible to find a modern fertility amulet that is still being employed in its primeval role – as an object carried on the body of a woman specifically to ensure pregnancy. The strange Triple Nut amulet is not a general-purpose good-luck charm. Its function is magically to increase the owner's chances of becoming pregnant and enjoying a successful birth.

Unlike so many amulets, the Triple Nut is not small enough to be worn as a piece of jewellery on a chain around the neck, or on the wrist or ankle. Made from a naturally growing triple nut and decorated with strips of leather, coloured beads and the occasional cowrie shell, each of these strange objects

weighs about 300g (10oz) and measures 13cm (5in) across. There is no loop, hook or point of attachment. The amulet is simply slipped into a fold of clothing and carried in the woman's costume. It is said that even to touch one fleetingly is likely to make a woman pregnant, and to carry one day after day is thought to be an absolute guarantee of fertility.

The symbolism of the Triple Nut is ambiguous. It can be viewed as a female torso, with featureless head and large, milk-filled breasts. Or it can be seen as stylized male genitals, with large testicles and a short penis. Either way, its essential feature is the paired spheres that form the most primitive and basic of all human sexual signals.

THE ACORN

BECAUSE IT COMES from the sacred oak tree, the acorn is believed to be endowed with special powers, and acorn amulets have been worn for many centuries. As a Body Guard it was reputed to protect against illness, especially against cholera.

A special feature of the oak tree was that, because its natural life-span was so much longer than that of a human being, it seemed to live for ever. As a result, it came to symbolize longevity. There was an old saying that 'an oak tree takes 200 years to grow, then stands still for 200 years and then takes 200 years to die'. This was an exaggeration, but the true life-span of this great tree was nevertheless an impressive 250 years. By association, therefore, the acorn became a symbol of long life and immortality. It was thought that if a woman carried one in her handbag she would be protected from ageing and never grow old.

In earlier times it was also believed that if an acorn was placed on a window-sill, the house would never be struck by lightning. This is why old-fashioned window-blinds had an acorn-shaped bobbin at the end of their pull-cords.

VERVAIN

THIS UNIMPRESSIVE little plant gained great significance in ancient times and was considered a magic herb in Persia, Greece, Rome and Britain. It was so sacred that the Druids insisted that anyone uprooting the plant should place honeycomb on the spot to atone for their action. In France it was known as the Herbe Sacrée; in Greece as the Holy Herb; in Wales as the Devil's Bane. It was frequently used against black magic, the ancient Romans putting it in their houses to ward off evil spirits.

The Persians believed that vervain would act as a lucky charm for those seeking affection. Under its magical influence, even an opponent would become friendly. The Romans adopted this superstition and their ambassadors often wore the plant when seeking an audience with an enemy leader. They also believed that displaying a small twig of vervain would protect its wearer from the Evil Eye.

More recent traditions have seen this plant as protective against poverty, nightmares, ageing, lightning and storms.

THE COCO DE MER

If you visit the Seychelles islands in the Indian Ocean today, you will find on sale in the shops there a small good-luck charm with a strangely sexual shape. It looks like the midsection of a female body, from waist to thighs. It is found nowhere else in the world and has a most curious history.

O<small>N THE ISLAND</small> of Praslin in the Seychelles archipelago there exists a unique, primeval valley. It is called the Vallée de Mai and was visited in 1881 by General Gordon of Khartoum. When he set eyes on it he was astounded by the strange fruits he saw there. They were massive double coconuts, each weighing 23kg (50lb) and containing the largest seeds in the world. It was not only their size that surprised him, but also their structure. In his own words, the shape of these gigantic nuts 'externally represents the heart, while the interior represents the thighs and belly [of a woman], which I consider as the seat of carnal desires'.

In an instant it all became clear to him – he was standing in the original Garden of Eden and all around him were none other than living examples of the Forbidden Fruit itself. If Eve had shown Adam one of these nuts instead of an innocent little apple, then the First Man would have had little doubt about which part of the First Woman was meant to be of interest to him.

The fact that the extraordinary double nut had a double symbolism – a heart-shape enclosing a female pelvis – made it even more impressive.

More amazing still, we now know that the 40m (130ft) tall trees that bear these forbidden fruits take longer to mature than a human being, the female trees not bearing fruit until they are 25 years old. Their nuts then take a further 7 years to grow and ripen. The trees themselves can each live for as long as 1,000 years, so that the ones standing today are, astonishingly, only a few generations removed from the original Tree of Knowledge.

The giant nuts are known by the name Coco de Mer, meaning 'sea-coconut'. They were given this title because, before their true origin was understood, it was believed that they came from a vast undersea palm tree.

In the 17th century, before their source was known and when very few had been seen by anyone in Europe, the Emperor of the Holy

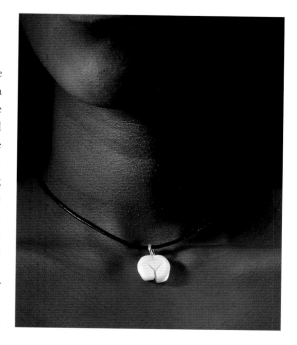

A miniature replica of the Coco de Mer, worn as an amulet today in the Seychelles.

Roman Empire, Rudolph II, offered the equivalent of 500 dairy cows for just one nut. They were so rare and so mysterious in those days, before the Vallée de Mai had been discovered, that when some of the nuts reached China they were used to fashion small magical amulets. This was probably their first use as Body Guards.

Because of the sexual associations of the nuts, their kernels are claimed to be powerful aphrodisiacs, and their erotic nature is amplified by the reproductive system of their trees. There are male trees, with phallic-shaped catkins 1m (3ft) long, and separate female trees that bear the huge fruits. The male and female trees stand close to one another and native legends insist that at night it is possible to hear them mating. In reality, the eerie sound is the rubbing and slapping together of the 6m (20ft) long palm fronds when a high wind blows.

It is little wonder that the remarkable Coco de Mer has become the subject of folklore and legend, and that today small images of this unique nut are still worn on a cord or chain around the neck as fertility symbols.

ROWAN

ACCORDING TO ANCIENT legend, the rowan tree is a powerful protector. It was said that only this kind of wood could be used to kill a vampire when driving a stake through its heart. As a Body Guard it was sacred to the goddess Brigit and was believed to be capable of breaking evil enchantments.

If carried as a protective amulet, a simple cross was fashioned by tying two small pieces of rowan together with a red ribbon. This was then hidden in a pocket or sometimes even sewn into the lining of an article of clothing.

On ships, rowan protects against storms; in the house, against lightning; on a grave, against haunting by the ghost of the departed. Planted near a house, it offered protection from ill fortune both for the occupants and for the building itself.

RUE

THIS UNUSUAL HERB proved to be too pungent and acrid for cooking, but was often planted near farm buildings housing domestic animals to protect them from the attacks of 'venomous beasts'. Also, the leaves of this plant used to be scattered over the floors of courtrooms to protect the judges from 'prison pestilence'. And soldiers, just before going into battle, were advised to smear the tips of their swords with the juice of rue leaves to make themselves invincible.

Curiously, rue's magical protective quality does have a basis in scientific fact. It has been discovered that if a leaf of rue is broken and crushed, the pungent odour released from its exposed juice does dramatically repel animals with sensitive noses, such as the cat. Some domestic cats begin to vomit after sniffing damaged rue leaves, and refuse to come near the plant on subsequent occasions. If planted in a garden, rue can therefore be used to repel cats in a non-magical, chemical way. This may explain why it was once so popular as a 'magical defence' around farm buildings.

ST JOHN'S WORT

THERE IS AN old saying that 'Trefoil, Vervain, John's Wort, Dill – Hinder witches of their will'. The most powerful herb for repelling evil forces was the one known as St John's Wort. To the Romans it was known as the Devil Chaser. Hanging it up in the house meant that the building and its occupants were magically protected and that, to quote an early author, 'then shall come no wicked spirit therein'. In addition to repelling the forces of evil, it offered additional protection from 'death by enchantment', and guarded the building from damage by thunderbolts and fire.

It was on the eve of the feast of St John the Baptist (24 June, which also happens to be Midsummer's Day) that the herb was most prominently displayed. On that night it was fixed over the front door, preventing the evil ones from entering the house. The herb was also known as the Flight of the Devil. In France it was called the All-holy or the Cure-all and in Ireland it was known as Mary's Glory.

The connection between this plant (*Hypericum*) and St John is based on the idea that, when the saint was beheaded, spots of his blood fell on its leaves and left red splashes on their surface. This belief arose from the fact that, if the leaves of one variety of the plant are held up to the light, it is possible to see translucent spots that appear red in colour.

THE FOUR-LEAF CLOVER

This is one of the most popular of all lucky charms. Each year in the United States four million four-leaf clovers are encased in glass or plastic, hung on chains and sold as protective pendants. There is even a Clover Specialty Company in Florida that has been supplying 'Genuine 4 Leaf Clovers…since 1939', and which now has its own Clovers Online website on the Internet.

THE ORDINARY THREE-leaf clover is said to be lucky (especially in Ireland, where it is known as the shamrock – see page 114), so it follows that the rare four-leaf version must be even luckier. Anyone who was fortunate enough to be wearing the 'four-branched leaf was safe from malicious enchantments'.

Like all good Body Guards, this one has acquired a colourful history. According to popular legend, Eve took a four-leaf clover with her when she left the Garden of Eden. Bearing in mind the size of clover, even a four-leaf clover, one can't help feeling that if this was an act of modesty her precaution was slightly flawed.

To occultists, this amulet was considered to be of great value because it enabled them to see hostile demons and therefore avoid them. It also protected against madness. To Christians it was thought to have special powers because the sacred cross had four parts. It was seen as a symbol of balance, unity and completeness.

In the 17th century, it was recorded that there was a custom of scattering four-leaf clovers before the bride to provide her with a little extra protection on her special day – a day that was so happy for all concerned that it would be certain to attract the malevolent attention of evil spirits.

There are different ways of treating the four-leaf clover when you find one. According to one source, you should hide it in your shoe to bring good fortune. Another says the best thing to do is to place it in a Bible. If a girl finds one, she will marry the next man she sees. Curiously, it is also claimed that if a man finds one and wears it, he will be able to avoid military service.

The four leaves have been given a variety of symbolic meanings. One authority claims that they stand for hope, faith, love and – the rare fourth leaf – luck. Another says that the quatrefoil motif they form is a 'world symbol' in which the four realms of north, east, south and west are implied by joined circles, with their four guardian spirits merged in the centre.

This German card wishes you a Happy New Year with the aid of fifteen four-leaf clovers to bring you good luck.

One saying goes: 'One leaf for fame, one leaf for wealth, one leaf for a faithful lover, and one leaf to bring you glorious health, all are in the four-leaf clover.' In a way, this sums up all the greatest fears of the vulnerable human being – fears about insignificance, poverty, sexual betrayal and ill-health. If wearing a humble little plant can help to avoid such major disasters then it is not surprising that enterprising salesmen can dispense with four million of them each year.

There are said to be even rarer forms of the clover leaf, with five, six or seven leaves. These have their own special protective values: the five-leaf brings riches, the six-leaf brings fame and the seven-leaf guards the wearer against all forms of evil. A rival view, however, sees these more extreme forms of clover as bringing only bad luck, so the jury is still out on the extremely rare multi-clovers.

THE SHAMROCK

A native of Ireland who is about to engage in a risky activity will traditionally seek the protective assistance of the lucky shamrock. That is why this particular form of Body Guard is so much in evidence at weddings and wars. Irish lovers used to exchange shamrocks at the time of their betrothal, and Irish soldiers carried them into battle. Today they are still widely used as lucky charms.

The shamrock is such a powerful good-luck charm that it has even been used as a motif on protective horse-brasses.

THE IRISH shamrock is a three-leaf clover. To be precise, it is the lesser yellow trefoil (*Trifolium repens minus*), a small form of the white clover (*Trifolium repens*). Other, related plants have sometimes been identified as 'shamrocks', but the lesser yellow trefoil is now generally accepted as the true one.

The trefoil pattern itself has been known as a protective device for many centuries. It appears to have started life in ancient India. From the Indus Valley civilization that flourished 5,000 years ago, there is a carved figure of a bearded man covered in 'shamrock' emblems. The same motif is encountered in the ancient art of Arabia and some have argued that the modern shamrock has derived its name from the Arabic *shamrakh*, an emblem of a triple-lunar goddess of pre-Islamic Arabs.

Much later, the trefoil appears as a pre-Christian amulet of the ancient Celts and its main centre seems to have been not Ireland but Wales. There it was entirely pagan in its magical role, its significance being related to the three heart-shaped leaves of the clover, which stood for the Triple Mothers, or 'Mother-hearts' of Celtic folklore. It was only later still that it was eventually taken over by the Christian Church, which (as it so often did with powerful pagan beliefs) decided to adopt it rather than oppose it.

According to Christian legend, it was St Patrick, Ireland's patron saint, who immortalized the shamrock as a sacred symbol. When he arrived in Ireland on a mission to convert the country to Christianity, he is said to have met with considerable opposition from a population who were devoted to their ancient sun-god. In presenting his case to King Leoghaire he is supposed to have plucked a shamrock and demonstrated to them that its three leaves represented the Holy Trinity.

Each year, on St Patrick's Day (17 March), the saint is honoured and shamrocks are displayed. In particular, they are worn during the popular ritual of 'drowning the shamrock'. This ancient custom appears to be an excuse to visit every public house within staggering distance and to give repeated liquid thanks to the shamrock for its protection during the past year. Puritanical minds were shocked by this, complaining that 'when they wet their shamrock, they often commit Excess in Liquor, which is not a right keeping of a Day to the Lord'.

So strongly did the shamrock become identified with Ireland ('Chosen leaf of bard and chief, Old Erin's chosen shamrock') that in the 18th century the country was sometimes jokingly referred to as Shamrockshire. For instance, 'Priests in Shamrockshire, they say, can women kiss, as well as pray.'

The Irish shamrock is used today as a pendant, a brooch or a pin, in the form of the original plant encased in glass or preserved in plastic, or as a gold or silver ornament. Many Irish emigrants have taken a shamrock with them when they left their native land, to keep a protective token of their home with them no matter where they may be. As a result, it is popular among the Irish not only in their native Ireland but also especially in the United States.

AMBER

A translucent, orange-brown, honey-coloured substance, amber is the fossilized resin of extinct pine trees. Strictly speaking, it must therefore be considered among the botanical Body Guards, although, because of the mineral form it takes, it has often been listed with the 'stones and rocks'.

T HE MAGICAL significance of amber has been aided by the fact that the bodies of small, ancient insects are often visible inside the resin, and when rubbed it develops a strong electric charge. In fact, the term 'electricity' is derived from the Greek word for amber (*electrum*).

Still employed today, Body Guards made of amber have been in use for centuries. Amber was thought to contain special powers that could be transferred to the wearer. As an amulet it has been used both as a powerful protection against bad luck and as a means of attracting good luck. It has also had a long reputation as a protection against diseases and ill-health. Pliny, the Roman author, mentions in his *Natural History*, written nearly 2,000 years ago, that 'a collar of Amber beads worn about the neck of young infants is a singular preservative to them against secret poison and a counter-charm for witchcraft and sorcery'.

According to the Egyptologist Wallis Budge, writing in 1888:

A model of the phallus made of amber was regarded as a most powerful protection against the Evil Eye and any and every attack of evil spirits…Beads made of amber preserved the wearer against…every kind of internal ailment. In many European countries amber is worn as a protection against witches and warlocks, and even ill-luck…In Eastern Asia amber amulets are made in the form of lions, hares, dogs, frogs, fish, etc, and these are believed to add to the virility of men and the fecundity of women.

In early days an amber amulet was immensely valuable. Pliny complained that an amber figurine was more expensive than a human slave.

As so often happens when endowing a substance with magical powers, early authors often felt the need to make amber sound more mysterious. They set about providing it with an exotic 'origin' and their far-fetched and misleading legends included the following:

The European Lynx, the urine of which was once thought to solidify to form amber.

- Amber is 'lynx stone' created from the solidified urine of the lynx.
- Amber is formed from the weeping of sun-nymphs (Heliads) on the occasion of the downfall of their brother (Phaethon). When he was struck by lightning they were turned into poplar trees which, instead of tears, every year wept a liquid that solidified to become amber.
- Amber is made of the solidified tears of the goddess Freya.
- Amber is a 'fatty sweat' washed up by the tide, and caused by the hot rays of the setting sun rebounding from the earth.
- Amber is formed from the tears of weeping birds.

Although these legends are no longer taken seriously, amber is still recommended as a valuable protective substance. As recently as 1997, the author of a book on 'crystal medicine' commented: 'Wear amber to attract warm, loyal and generous people in your life.' Even in a scientific age, ancient beliefs are stubborn survivors.

117

THE LUCKY BEAN

THE LUCKY BEAN amulet originated in India, but its popularity eventually spread to the West. Always a minor Body Guard, the little red bean was pierced and added to a bead necklace to bring the wearer good luck and protection from 'evil sorcerers'. In a more elaborate version, a hole was cut in it and the centre of the bean hollowed out to receive a small ivory elephant. The elephant gave the amulet a double impact.

In one tradition it is said that if a couple quarrel, the women should carry three lima beans, strung on a silk thread, for two days and the quarrel will end. It is also claimed that, for a man, carrying a pair of beans as a protective amulet will prevent or cure impotency. This appears to be because the beans resemble a man's testicles.

A special kind of lucky bean is found in the Far East. This is the large Sea Bean, favoured by Japanese fishermen, who find them floating in the ocean, scoop them up and keep them as lucky charms. In appearance, they are shiny, flat, circular and dark brown, with an average width of about 5cm (2in). Despite their name, they are not true beans, but hard seeds that are occasionally shed into the waves and washed out to sea. Their special appeal is that they are long-lasting, mysterious objects, ideally suited to becoming 'discovered' marine amulets.

As with many other lucky charms, the fact that Sea Beans are found, rather than bought, makes them more effective as protective amulets. It has often been pointed out that if you buy, say, a horseshoe or a rosary, its purchase will rob it of its magical properties. The best amulets are always ones that are found, made or received as gifts. To the superstitious mind, paying money for an object somehow sterilizes it and reduces it to a commercial possession robbed of its mystical forces.

MANDRAKE

THE MANDRAKE IS A Mediterranean plant with a forked, fleshy root. The shape of this root is reminiscent of the human body and this resemblance has led to many strange beliefs. One of these states that any man who pulls a mandrake from the ground will be driven mad by the agonized shriek of the plant as it is uprooted. To overcome this, mandrake collectors went to amazing lengths. One method was to tie one end of a piece of string to the mandrake and the other end to a hungry dog. The collector would then throw a piece of meat near the dog and quickly cover his ears to block out the lethal scream of the plant. The dog would struggle towards it, uprooting the mandrake in the process. The roots of the mandrakes became valued amulets, protecting their female owners from infertility. So valuable were they to sterile women that there was a roaring trade in clever fakes made from the roots of white bryony, cut into human shapes. Seeds were inserted into small cuts made in the 'pubic' region and the fake roots were buried until these seeds had started to germinate. They were then dug up and trimmed with a sharp knife, creating what looked like suggestive tufts of 'hair'.

Over the years, the mandrake has acquired many colourful names, such as the Love Apple, Satan's Apple, Apple of the Fool, the Devil's Testicles, Phallus of the Field, Eggs of the Genie, Ladykins, Brain Thief, Sorcerer's Root and The Hand of Glory.

Sometimes called the Witches' Mannikin, the mandrake takes many strange forms.

OTHER PLANT AMULETS

Ebony

Black ebony wood is believed to be protective and is therefore frequently used in making amulets, especially those to guard against the Evil Eye. In Latin America this kind of wood is particularly popular as the material from which small Figgas (fig-sign hands) are carved. These amulets are given to children to defend them against evil spirits. So magical is this kind of wood that wands made of ebony are said to provide magicians with 'pure, unadulterated power'.

Fern

Carried as a lucky amulet, fern is said to have the power of guiding the wearer to great treasures. In the house, it is often added to flower arrangements because of its protective powers. This is why it is often seen among the decorations at weddings. In some countries fern is planted near the front doorstep of a house to protect it from evil spirits trying to enter the home. In addition, fern is also believed to protect against drought, snakes, poverty, sickness, toothache and ageing.

Common marigolds are used to protect the house from evil.

Marigold

Marigold is said to symbolize the mystic gold of the Virgin Mary. It has sometimes been called Holigolde or Marygold. If you are summoned to court, it is believed that carrying protective marigold in your pocket will ensure that you are justly treated and that the judge's decision will favour you. This flower has also been employed to protect the house against evil spirits. To prevent them from entering the home, garlands of marigolds are strung around the door. To make dreams come true and protect the sleeper, it is scattered under the bed.

Marjoram

Marjoram is another flower that has been carried as an amulet to keep the wearer safe from evil spirits. More specifically, it has been employed as a defence against depression. In the winter it is also worn to protect against colds and other ailments. Marjoram defends the home against evil when a small, fresh piece of it is placed in each room. If it is grown in the garden it is supposed to throw a protective shield around the house.

Marjoram has the reputation of curing depression.

120

Thyme

Thyme has been carried to protect the wearer from cowardice, lack of energy, ill-health and the loss of psychic powers. Hidden beneath the pillow, it is also said to have the power of protecting the sleeper from nightmares. Women who wear a sprig of thyme in their hair will supposedly be lucky in love.

White heather

White heather, as distinct from the more common purple heather, is worn as a luck-bringer and also to protect against violent crimes, especially rape. Many people, on finding it growing wild at the roadside, stop and pick small sprigs to wear in their buttonholes, or to decorate their cars, in the hope that it will bring them good fortune. White heather is also reputed to possess a virtue similar to that of amethyst – namely that, as a protective amulet, it

A decorative brooch converted into a lucky charm by its white heather motif.

Thyme is reputed to prevent nightmares.

prevents drunkenness. It achieves this in a slightly different way, however. Whereas amethyst allows its owner to drink without getting drunk, white heather stops the alcoholic from drinking in the first place.

Wormwood

Although it is no more than a common roadside plant, found throughout Europe, wormwood has been highly valued as a medicinal herb since ancient times. Its aid to those suffering from 'surfets' (hangovers) and a variety of other internal conditions led to its use for many centuries as a panacea. In addition to its medicinal functions, it was also employed as a charm. The dead roots of the plant were known as Wormwood Coral, and it was believed that if a piece of this was placed under the pillow of a loved one, it would induce amorous dreams that would intensify their love.

Heaven Help Us
RELIGIOUS BODY GUARDS

For those who follow a religious creed it is possible to put their trust in a sacred amulet that symbolizes their faith. Simply to wear it on their body, or place it in view, is to call upon all the power and influence of the god or gods that they recognize, requesting their assistance in facing the trials of the day. For Christians there are crucifixes and St Christophers; for the Sikhs there is the Kara; for Muslims the Crescent; for Jews the Star of David; and for Buddhists the Laughing Buddha. For those who feel the need for the mystical aid of some supernatural force, but who do not subscribe to a modern mainstream religion, there are some appealing alternatives that revive more ancient beliefs – such as the Egyptian Ankh and the Tau, the Chinese Pi Disc and the Viking Thor's Hammer.

ST CHRISTOPHER

By far the most popular Body Guard for travellers is the St Christopher. Even today there are countless people who will not set off on a journey – even a short one – without their St Christopher medallion attached to a chain around their neck, tucked safely into a purse, wallet or handbag, or hanging up in their car. It is believed that anyone who sets eyes upon the image of the saint will not die on that day.

St Christopher crossing the river, by Giovanni Bellini (c.1468).

SURPRISINGLY FOR such a widely used amulet, we know very little about St Christopher himself. His legend, briefly, is as follows:

He was a strong, ugly, bearded, 'dog-faced' giant of a man, who is usually shown carrying a staff. His original name was Offero, although he was also sometimes referred to as Reprobus. He came from Canaan, where he was working for a powerful king. When he discovered that his great king was frightened of the Devil he decided to change his allegiance and went to work for the Devil instead. Then, one day, he noticed that the Devil himself was afraid of someone called Christ, so he went in search of this most powerful of all kings. He failed to find him but was told by a hermit that his best chance of doing so was to live alone by a dangerous river and to help people across it.

Offero followed this advice and for some time lived alone by a ford in a strongly flowing river. He carried travellers across, which he did with ease, since he was between 5 and 7 metres (18 and 22 feet) high. But then one day a small boy came to the river-bank and asked for his help. He put the child on his shoulders and waded into the water. When he was halfway across the river, he began to suffer from the enormous weight of the child and thought they would drown. The child explained to Offero that he was a heavy load because he himself was carrying the whole world on *his* shoulders. As soon as Offero understood this and recognized that the child was Christ and that Christ was supporting the whole world, the boy vanished.

This simple parable is clearly meant to indicate that an acceptance of the power of Christ will remove a great burden from your shoulders, but it tells us remarkably little about St Christopher himself. Historically, it has been recorded that he was martyred in the third century, when he was beheaded for refusing to honour the Roman gods. This is supposed to have happened in Lycia, in Asia Minor, under the Roman Emperor Decius around the year AD 250. Beyond that, little is known and the Church authorities recently decided that perhaps he was no more than an attractive 12th-century fiction. As a result, he was struck off the official list of saints in 1969 and his Saint's Day (25 July in the West, 9 March in the East) was removed from the Universal Calendar. Such is his appeal, however, that popular opinion has completely ignored his demotion. His amulet continues to be worn as a protection against the many very real hazards of modern travel.

And so, St Christopher, whose name is derived from the Greek Christophoros, which means literally 'Christ-bearer', remains to this day the patron saint of travellers all over the world. He is most popular among the Catholics of North America, Mexico, Ireland and (despite the Vatican's downgrading of him) Italy. In addition, in earlier days, an amulet of the saint was said to protect against plague, tempest and water.

In the United States in the 1970s a new fashion developed which saw the St Christopher medallion become a token of romantic attachment between a boy and a girl. When they fell in love, each would give the other a St Christopher necklace. As well as the medallion's traditional function of offering protection during travels it became a public display of being promised to someone. If the relationship ended, the necklaces would be returned. This practice began in the surf culture of southern California and quickly spread across North America.

THE ANKH

The ancient Egyptian Ankh, a cross with a loop at the top, represented the 'imperishable vital force' and is still worn as a protective amulet today. Often referred to simply as a 'symbol of life', it is also called the Crux Ansata, and is seen as a 'relative' of the Christian cross, although it predates that image by many centuries.

A NYONE EXPECTING that, because it has such a simple design, the Ankh must be a straightforward symbol must brace themselves for a shock, for in reality this turns out to be one of the most complicated and confusing images in the history of art.

As a protective amulet, the Ankh is said to guard the wearer (or carrier) against sickness, infertility and a loss of psychic powers. It is also said to offer the wearer immortality, if not in this world then at least in the next. Curiously though, the 'immortality' that it offers in the afterlife falls just short of eternity, being limited to a mere 'hundred thousand million years'.

The shape of the Ankh has been interpreted variously as the 'tree of life', a phallus, a hand-mirror in its case, a magical knot or the sun rising above the horizon. It has also been explained as a combination of signs representing the male and female genitals, and this has been given as the reason for its use as a fertility symbol. Alternatively, it is thought – rather incongruously – to depict the tie-straps of an Egyptian sandal. The reason for this last interpretation is that the hieroglyph for a sandal-strap has the same design.

Others see the Ankh as a magic key – the Key of Life, the Key of the Nile or, more exotically, the Key of Knowledge of the Mysteries and Hidden Wisdom. For some, the key is 'an instrument to unlock the Gates of Death', which explains why the Ankh is

Some Ankhs today are created in gold as expensive fashion accessories.

The Ankh has recently shown a resurgence in popularity as an alternative to the Christian cross.

associated with immortality. Following on from this idea, some scholars interpret the loop at the top of the Ankh as a sign of eternity, with the lines running from it acting as extensions sideways and downwards. In other words, they view it as an extended eternity.

One ingenious theory sees the Ankh as a sheet of papyrus rolled into a scroll and then tied with a strip of papyrus. The idea behind this last explanation is that on this papyrus a sacred spell is written and it is these words that comprise the active protective element.

The truth is that nobody really knows *what* the Ankh represents, only that it was of immense significance to the ancient Egyptians and provided them with their most popular amulet. In fact, its popularity was so great that it was the only Egyptian amulet to be adopted by the Copts as an early Christian symbol. In the British Museum there is a remarkable Coptic amulet showing the Virgin Mary holding a Christian cross in one hand and an Ankh in the other. Eventually, of course, the Ankh did lose ground and the Christian cross came to be totally dominant, as the doctrine of Jesus Christ spread to become a world force in religion.

Only in very recent times have people in the West, with a resurgence of romantic interest in ancient beliefs, come to re-adopt the ancient Egyptian Ankh as a fashionable amuletic device, the ideal 'alternative cross'.

THE LAUGHING BUDDHA

THE BUDDHIST RELIGION, which began about 2,500 years ago in northern India, spread rapidly throughout Asia. It is estimated that there are about 500 million Buddhists alive today, and in some regions, especially Thailand, it is a common practice to wear a small Buddha amulet. Known as the Pha, this popular Body Guard shows the seated, cross-legged, smiling, long-eared, round-faced, overweight, pot-bellied figure of the 'Laughing Buddha'. He is considered to be extremely lucky and, in particular, is believed to protect from sudden death all those who wear his image.

The Laughing Buddha, also known as the Maitreya Buddha, or the Buddha of the Future, is a symbol of happiness, kindness and innocent joy. He is thought to bring great wealth and was the patron saint of goldsmiths in ancient China. His round belly is seen as a physical representation of his happiness and wealth, presumably reflecting the idea

that he can afford to eat well and that he enjoys his food. It is said that if you rub his belly once a day you will increase your chances of sharing his good fortune.

In recent years, the fame of the Laughing Buddha amulet has spread far and wide, and today it can be found in Central and North America and Europe as well as in much of Asia.

In 1998 an accident occurred on the streets of Bangkok when a police motorcyclist guarding the Prime Minister's motorcade struck a passing car. Later that day the Prime Minister visited the injured policeman in hospital and, according to a Bangkok newspaper, asked him: 'What Buddha amulet do you wear?' It is not clear from this whether he meant that the policeman's amulet had saved him from death, or that, had he worn a better one, he might have been spared the accident altogether. But what is certainly clear is that, in Thailand at least, this particular amulet still has a very high profile.

PADMA SAMBHAVA

PADMA SAMBHAVA is regarded as one of the founders of Tibetan Buddhism, and his image is worn as a protective amulet by many Tibetans. To some devout Tibetans he is the 'second Buddha'. His name means 'One Born of a Lotus' and, according to legend, he emerged as a boy from a lotus in the Indus river.

He was an Indian mystic and magician who was renowned for his triumph in defeating demonic powers – a reputation that would later make him the perfect subject for a protective amulet.

In the eighth century he was invited by the Tibetan king to help establish Buddhism in that country. The conversion was already under way, but the local demons (the gods of the older, local Bon religion) were said to be resisting, so Padma Sambhava was called in to use his remarkable powers to defeat them. He succeeded by cleverly co-opting them and enrolling them as the protectors of the new teachings.

Padma Sambhava personified the more colourful, magical form of Tibetan Buddhism, in contrast to other, more scholarly, monastic traditions. These two strands could never be entirely at ease with one another, but they did manage to work together, one satisfying the supernatural leanings of the followers of the earlier, more primitive Bon religion and the other bringing order and scholarship.

It is clear from this why it is the amuletic figure of Padma Sambhava that should have become such a popular Body Guard in Tibet. He was protecting people from evil spirits in the eighth century, and over 1,000 years later his amulet is still carrying out the same duties.

It is a tribute to his persistence as a supernatural force that despite the Chinese invasion of Tibet and the attempted suppression of Tibetan Buddhism, these small amulets are today still being fashioned in silver by the Newari people in the Katmandu Valley.

THE CHRISTIAN CROSS

Amulets of the Christian cross, with or without the figure of the crucified Christ showing on the front, have been worn for centuries as protective devices, usually on cords or chains around the neck. Technically, only those displaying the crucified figure should be called crucifixes, but this distinction is not always made.

CHRISTIAN CROSSES THAT do not include the tortured figure are more popular, more widespread and much more variable in their design. (They first appeared in the fourth century.) The true crucifixes (which did not appear until the eighth century) tend to be highly traditional and realistic, but the others vary from the simplest of plain crosses to the amazingly elaborate and complicated. The most ornate of all – so much so that they are barely identifiable as crosses – are the carrying crosses from Ethiopia.

According to one authority, no fewer than 285 different kinds of cross have been worn at one time or another, by those who wish to enlist the spiritual strength of Christ to protect them. The cross appears in gold, silver, stone and crystal, and many other materials. In pure numbers, worldwide, it must certainly be the most common of all Body Guards. Even in Western circles where belief in God is on the wane, the cross manages to survive, if only as a chic form of body adornment or fashion accessory. If one stops to think about it, it is curious that an instrument of torture should have become such a revered image.

Most of the time, as an amulet, the cross simply hangs on the chest of its owner, quietly proclaiming its protective presence. Occasionally, however, it is thrust into a more active role. As any cinema-goer knows, this is dramatically demonstrated in every vampire horror film, when the hero makes the sign of the cross, usually improvised with his forearms or two pieces of wood, to repel the advancing bloodsucker. When priests are threatened, they usually hold their crucifixes forward, towards the source of danger, displaying the face of the cross to the evil one.

A silver cross showing one of the many complex designs popular in Ethiopia.

There has long been a tradition in which an illiterate person puts his or her name to a document with a cross. This is sometimes seen as 'the best that they can do', but there is more to it than that. By making their cross, the person signing is placing a protective symbol on the document to guard it and its contents from evil. They are, in effect, transferring their personal 'amulet' to the sheet of paper.

One of the most bizarre forms of protective crucifix was recently put on sale to the Christian clergy. It consists of a boxy, three-dimensional cross which contains an electronic panic alarm. At the press of a button it emits a two-tone shriek similar to a car alarm. This high-tech crucifix, designed to deter inner-city thieves and muggers, adds an extremely practical, secular form of protection to the more spiritual plea for heavenly help that supposedly emanates from all clerical crosses.

The oddity of this panic-alarm cross is exceeded only by the new protective role of the crucifixes of the pious nuns of St Anne's Convent in Madras. These hard-working sisters, struggling to bring Christian kindness to the back streets of India, had been raped so many times that they were driven to the extreme measure of hiring a martial arts expert to train them in self-defence. One of his tactics was to persuade them to carry their metal crucifixes in their closed hands, with the pointed end of the cross protruding through their bent fingers. In this way they could use them as holy 'knuckle-dusters' to protect themselves from their brutal attackers.

Eastern crosses of this kind were worn as charms against sickness and accidents.

THE EARLY CROSS

It may come as a surprise to devout Christians to learn that, thousands of years before Christ was crucified, small crosses were being worn around the neck as protective amulets. They were popular in ancient Cyprus in the Chalcolithic period between 4000 BC and 2500 BC. The one shown here is a plain, undecorated cross made of pale green soapstone (picrolite) and was provided with a loop-hole for suspension.

As we have no written records from such an early period, we can only guess at the way these crosses were supposed to protect their wearers, but there are some important clues. The plain crosses were part of a series of small amulets, some of which are more detailed and therefore more revealing. The most elaborate of them show a female figure with her knees bent up and her arms stretched out sideways. This squatting position suggests that she is being shown at the moment of giving birth and it has been argued that these little stone figurines would have been worn by women as fertility charms to encourage an easy birth or simply to increase their chances of getting pregnant. In one famous example, the female figure is actually shown wearing one of the small figurines around her own neck, emphasizing how important it was to display such an amulet.

A Chiastolite or cross-stone marked with a naturally occurring cross, used for protection.

be purely coincidental that, several thousand years later, similar crosses were worn by Christians for their own protective reasons. Or perhaps the tradition of wearing protective crosses lasted long enough to influence the early Christians in their move to adopting this symbol as their own. We may never know, but the existence of these very early, Copper Age crosses on the island of Cyprus does, at least, show us how potent the simple cruciform figure has proved to be in the world of protective charms and amulets.

There are several intermediate stages between the detailed representation of the female figure and the simple cross. In descending order of detail, these stages are as follows:

1 Figure showing feet, bent knees, outstretched arms, pendant around neck, and head with eyes, nose, hair.
2 Figure showing feet, bent knees, outstretched arms, and head with eyes, nose, hair.
3 Figure showing feet, bent knees, outstretched arms and head.
4 Figure showing feet, outstretched arms and head.
5 Figure showing outstretched arms and head.
6 Figure showing outstretched arms, ie a cross.

When viewed in this sequence it is obvious that the crosses are highly simplified and stylized representations of a human female giving birth. It may

A cruciform figure wearing an amulet of herself, fashioned in Cyprus over 4,000 years ago.

THE TAU

T HE TAU, SHAPED like a capital T, was an ancient symbol found in Egypt, the Middle East and parts of western Europe. It stood for wisdom, power, life, regeneration and fecundity and was often worn as a protective charm. More specifically it was used to guard against skin diseases, snake-bite, poison and injury in times of war. When the Romans were holding a roll-call after a battle, to see who was still alive, a Tau was marked down against the name of any soldier who answered, symbolizing the fact that he had been protected from death.

Some authorities claimed that this T-shape was the true design of the cross on which Christ died, but the idea did not find favour and was largely abandoned, probably because the Tau was widely known to be so much older than Christianity itself.

Today the Tau is seldom encountered except in the modified form of the gavel or mallet used by judges, auctioneers and committee chairmen when protecting their authority. It may have travelled this route because it was identified by some with the hammer of Thor, the Nordic thunder-god.

The Tau was worn in ancient times as a protection against disease and snake-bite.

A rare Anglo-Saxon ivory Tau crosier from the British Museum, dated at circa AD 1030.

THOR'S HAMMER

THE MOST POPULAR amulet in Scandinavia is the magical hammer of Thor, the thunder-god of the Vikings. Armed with this wonderful stone weapon Thor was the Great Protector, waging terrible war on all hostile forces, especially the Ice and Snow Giants of the North. As his chariot rumbled through the sky, claps of thunder were heard. And when he struck down his enemies, his hammer-blows were visible as shafts of lightning.

Thor's mighty hammer, known as Mjolnir ('the Destroyer'), never missed its mark and magically returned to his hand after its damage was done. In more peaceful moments it was used to solemnize marriages and became the protective symbol of married couples.

Thor may seem remote from us today, but we do unthinkingly use his name every Thursday, which is Thor's day. (In ancient Germany, Thor was known as Donar, and in the German language Thursday is *Donnerstag*.)

For over 1,000 years, Thor's hammer has been worn as a small pendant hung on a cord around the neck. It is still popular in Scandinavia today, although it has recently attracted some political controversy in Sweden, where young men with an extreme right-wing bias have started wearing it as a symbol of their group. To some Swedes this has given the hammer a slightly racist flavour, but for most it remains too famous as a symbol of Scandinavian culture to be hijacked by any political faction. As a result it is still widely sold as a protective charm.

Modern examples can be found in gold, silver, brass and cornelian. Some are complex, detailed copies of ancient examples; others are highly stylized, smoothly simplified versions. There is also a special version described as *Tor's Magiska Amulett* ('Thor's Magic Amulet'). This is a triple amulet consisting of a ring from which hang a small hammer, a flint-striker for making fire and a 'cutter for the harvest'. Together these three offer respectively, Thor's protection from enemies, cold and hunger.

THE CRESCENT

The crescent is a symbol of the new moon and offers the protection of the moon-goddess.

It is sometimes confused with two other amulets – the horns and the horseshoe. Each is

based on a U-shape and sometimes one is said to carry the message of the others.

IN ANCIENT EGYPT the crescent was the symbol of the goddess Isis and was used to protect mothers and children. In Rome young women wore silver crescents to ensure that they produced healthy babies and to protect themselves from witchcraft, delusions, hysteria and failure in love. Its strong association with newborn children derives from the fact that the crescent is the small, 'newborn' moon. (It was always the waxing moon, never the waning moon.) And its association with women derives from the fact that, like them, it repeatedly passes through a regular monthly cycle. Because the lunar deity was seen as female, calling for her protection was viewed as madness by the male-dominated early Christian Church. The term 'lunatic' for a mad person derives from this association.

A crescent with a single star between its points is also the protective symbol of Turkey, appearing on its flag. Its use in this context dates back to the moment in the mid-15th century when the Turks first took Constantinople and found this particular image at the base of a statue of Isis who, as Hecate, had previously been the guardian of the city.

Despite its feminine gender, the crescent image has spread to become a widely known Islamic symbol. It appears not only on the Turkish flag, but on the flags of Algeria, Azerbaijan, the Comoros, Malaysia, the Maldives, Mauritania, Pakistan, Tunisia and Turkmenistan – all Islamic countries. This seems curious when one remembers that the Muslim faith is, like Christianity, a male-dominated religion. Its masculine leaders have inevitably modified the original form of goddess

In one version of this amulet, the crescent is held by a hand.

worship, with the old moon-mother of pre-Islamic Arabia, whose name was Al-Lat, being masculinized to Al-Lah, but somehow the female crescent has escaped this kind of sexist transformation and has managed to survive.

Today crescent-shaped amulets are still sometimes offered for sale in the West, but they are not especially popular and are more likely to be merely decorative rather than protective. The nearest that most Westerners come to employing this image is at breakfast time when they devour a crescent-shaped pastry once used as a sacred offering to the moon-goddess, but now known simply as a croissant.

Sasanian necklace (AD 250–650) with a pendant in the form of a large crescent.

THE THUNDERBOLT

IN TIBET, INDIA and Nepal there is a strange, magic wand called the Dorje or Vajra which is used in religious rituals. Known in the West as the thunderbolt, it has a complex history and confused symbolism. Its basic shape is that of a double-headed mace or a dumb-bell – a handle with a knob at each end. It has been described as:

- ♣ a symbol of power and indestructibility
- ♣ a symbol of the male principle – the penis
- ♣ a weapon of the gods – a sacred club
- ♣ a symbol of 'lightning strike' as maximum active energy
- ♣ a rain-maker

In its latter capacity, one legend describes the thunderbolt overpowering some serpents who are causing a drought. They have swallowed all the waters but the thunderbolt forces them to disgorge them, in this way bringing fertilizing rain.

Many thunderbolts, made of bronze, are too big and heavy to be carried as protective amulets. They are the prized possessions of monks and magicians, and are employed extensively in sacred rituals. But they are also found in a small, portable form, only about 7cm (a few inches) long, that can be worn as a pendant. In this role, they are used to defend the wearer against harmful magic and evil spirits. They also offer their owners promise of abundance, fertility and riches.

THE WHEEL

FROM ANCIENT TIMES the symbol of the turning wheel has been linked to the endless cycles of the heavens. The wheel represents the universe: the wheel is the power of the sun; the wheel is the support of the great chariot that drives the sun through the sky; the wheel is the attribute of the sun-god, its hub being the sun itself and its spokes the sun's rays shining down; and the wheel is rebirth and renewal.

It is all of these things and more, so it is little wonder that from the earliest epochs the wheel has been employed as a powerful amulet, giving its owner the protection of the greatest forces of nature. To wear the image of a wheel is to be guarded by the mighty sun-god himself.

In another capacity, the turning of the wheel was controlled by the wheel-goddess that the Romans called Fortuna, who supervised the changing seasons and decided the fates of men. But over the centuries Fortuna's wheel shrank in size and power, becoming demoted to the Wheel of Fortune of gamblers and gamesters, and then the roulette wheel. Finally, it reached rock-bottom as the tawdry gimmick of a television game-show. The great goddess Fortuna has become Lady Luck.

Despite this decline, the symbolic wheel has survived. It may not be one of the most popular of amulets, but it is nevertheless an image that turns up from time to time in a wide variety of cultures and will probably continue to do so.

THE KARA

A follower of the Sikh religion feels unprotected without a symbolic Body Guard in the form of a metal bangle called the Kara. This religious bracelet, worn permanently on the right wrist, must be made of iron or steel. It is forbidden to fashion it from either gold or silver.

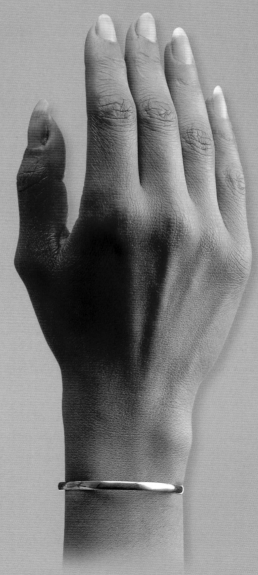

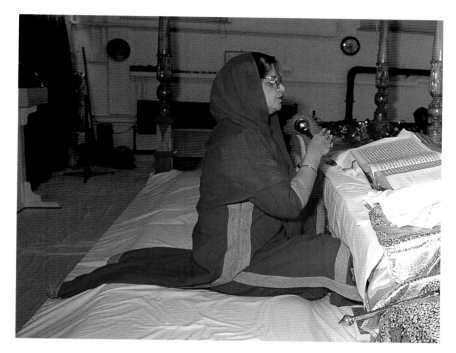

To a Sikh, the Kara is a permanent, life-long companion of great significance.

SIKHS IN THE WEST today sometimes find that their strict insistence on being able to wear this symbolic ornament at all times creates unusual problems for them. In 1998 a Sikh woman who refused to take off her Kara claimed that she suffered discrimination in the English food factory where she worked. The management had banned 'jewellery' on the food production line because of possible contamination from germs, and demanded that she remove it. This would have meant cutting through it, but even if it had been easy to slip off she would not have done so because of her obedience to religious custom. There was an impasse. Neither side would give in, so she was moved to another part of the factory.

Noticing that the other women on the food production line were allowed to wear their wedding rings, she lodged a formal discrimination complaint. At the tribunal hearing she commented:

'A wedding ring is also a magnet for germs, so what they are saying about the Kara is just rubbish. The Kara is very important to Sikhs – we believe it protects us from evil and temptation.'

This is undoubtedly the way that Sikhs view the role of the Kara although, officially, its function is to act as a symbol of strength and unity. The iron or steel represents the strength, and the circular shape, with no beginning and no end, symbolizes the unity. But clearly Sikhs who wear the Kara see it as a protective device, without which they would be at risk.

So important is the Kara to Sikhs that its name even rates a special mention in the British Laws of Association Football. The 1996–7 Amendments to the Laws state: 'Referees should ensure that players should not wear articles which may constitute a danger to other players or themselves…Referees, however, should make allowances for religious symbols (eg a player of the Sikh religion wearing a Kara in a match) providing they are not dangerous and adequate covering be applied as protection.'

It is interesting that one of the tenets of the Sikh religion is that 'it admits of no idols or superstitions'. Officially, the Kara is 'symbolic' rather than 'protective'. Unofficially, however, it is worn just like any other amulet – to keep its wearer safe from evil.

THE PI DISC

IF YOU VISIT THE Chinese market in Singapore and ask for a lucky charm, the amulet you are most likely to be offered is of a surprisingly simple shape. It is a circular, flat disc of jade with a hole in the middle. This, you are told, is the Chinese symbol of heaven known as a Pi disc (sometimes called a Bi disc) and will protect you at times of difficulty. When you anticipate trouble, to protect yourself from it you must rub the disc with your fingers and keep on rubbing it until the danger has passed.

This tradition of the protective Pi disc is centuries old. In fact, in China it can be traced back to neolithic times, 5,000 years ago. One tomb dating from the fourth millennium BC contained no fewer than 24 Pi discs, which had been placed on the body as 'protectors of the dead'. Clearly the friends of the occupant of that tomb were determined that he would get to heaven.

To Western eyes it seems strange to envisage heaven with a hole in the middle, rather like a flattened Polo mint. The official explanation given is that 'the hole in this circular image of space signifies the path of transcendence'. In other words, you get to heaven by passing through the hole in the middle of the flat disc. By staring hard at the shape of the disc you can imagine yourself rising up through the aperture and into the skies above.

In addition to being used as tomb offerings to assist the dead in their passage to the afterlife, these ceremonial discs were also employed by the early Chinese emperors during court rituals that involved making animal sacrifices to heaven. Today they may have lost their lofty status and descended to the level of popular lucky charms, but by their very simplicity they manage to retain a strangely mysterious quality that leaves a lasting impression on all who handle them.

Although modern Pi discs cost very little when sold at Eastern market stalls, the older ones are highly valued today and can fetch large sums when sold at auction. Some of the finest examples break with the usual 'minimalist' Pi tradition and show exquisitely carved dragons on their rims.

THE SEAL OF SOLOMON

SOLOMON'S SEAL WAS an all-powerful amulet in ancient times and was worn for protection against all forms of danger, misfortune and evil. Also known as the Interlaced Triangle, or the Hexagram, it consists of two triangles, one pointing up and one down, which together form a six-pointed star.

It has been in use for thousands of years and in more recent times, as the Star of David, the Shield of David or the Magen Dawid, it has become widely known as the emblem of Judaism.

In ancient India, the two triangles were male and female. The upward-pointing one was the god Shiva and the downward one was the goddess Kali. They were intertwined together in a state of permanent sexual union. It was from this magical union that all life in the universe was believed to arise.

The upward, male element also symbolized fire and the downward, female element stood for water – the fire of heaven fertilizing the female 'deep'. (Amusingly, their combination – fire-water – led to its use as a symbol of brandy.)

The upward-pointing triangle has also been called 'all that is good' and the downward-pointing one 'all that is evil', with the two together representing the triumph of good over evil.

The three sides of the upper triangle represent the sacred trinity that is the central concept of several major religions. Examples of these trinities are:

RELIGION	SACRED TRINITY
Ancient Egyptian	*Osiris, Isis and Horus*
Hindu	*Brahma, Vishnu and Shiva*
Buddhist	*The Buddha, the Dharma and the Sangha*
Druid	*The Mystic Three*
Christian	*The Father, the Son and the Holy Ghost*
In general terms	*Love, truth and wisdom*

The three sides of the lower triangle represent the World, the Flesh and the Devil; or alternatively Envy, Hatred and Malice.

143

THE ROSARY

The act of prayer is frequently used as a protective ritual. People ask their God to take care of them and save them from danger. In many countries it has been the habit for centuries to count prayer-beads as a form of devotion. There is a simple reason for this. If the same prayer has to be recited over and over again for a set number of times, it is difficult to keep the score and to know when a prayer cycle has been completed.

THE ROSARY has a long history. In the early days, a piece of string with knots tied at intervals down its length was employed. With each prayer the string (held in the hand) was advanced by one knot. When the end of the string was reached the prayer cycle was ended. A more popular version of this saw the string tied in a circle. The next step was to replace the knots with beads. By having one large bead, a tassel, or some other special detail at one point in the circle, it was possible to tell when the 'counting of the beads' had gone full circle.

This object, the rosary, has for many people become more than a mere religious device, an aid to prayer. It has become a precious, jealously guarded amulet in its own right. The evil it protects against can be of several kinds. It can vary from moral temptation to witchcraft, or from physical illness to a thunderstorm. St Catherine of Sienna and St Bridget of Sweden used rosaries to heal the sick. Polish peasants walk three times round the house with bell and candle and rosary to ward off lightning. In southern Italy, the beads of the rosary are used to remove the evil spirits from a man who has become impotent. And a special kind of rosary, known as the Austrian 'Need Beads', is used for the protection of children from sickness and the Evil Eye.

In the West, most people think of rosaries as Catholic accessories, but this is only a part of their story. Surprisingly, the earliest mention of a circle of prayer-beads occurs in India, where it was at first associated with the cult of Shiva.

From being the attribute of certain Shivaite monks, the rosary gradually extended its range and was adopted by Jainism and Buddhism. From contact with India it spread to Tibet and China, and from China to Japan. Also from contact with India, Persians and Arabs acquired the rosary. Christian

The infant Jesus playing with the Virgin's rosary beads, in a 16th-century painting by Joos van Cleve.

prayer-counters started to appear from about AD 1000.

The precise number of beads on a rosary varies from religion to religion, depending on the number of prayers that must be said to complete a cycle. Catholics must say 150 prayers and their rosaries are divided up into 15 sets of 10 beads. Each set of ten is separated from the next by a larger bead and, at one point in the ring there will be a special punctuation, probably in the form of a crucifix, to mark the end of the cycle. For common use, there is a 'lesser rosary' of only 50 beads, in which each of the beads is worth three prayers.

Of the other religions, the Greek Orthodox rosary (called a *kombologion*, or counting-string) has 103 knots (four groups of 25 standard beads separated by three large beads and a pendant). The Russian Orthodox rosary (called a *vervitsa*) also has 103 knots, or sometimes beads, but here the four groups are of different sizes (17, 40, 12 and 33).

In Tibet, Burma, China and Japan, the Buddhist rosaries nearly always have 108 beads. So does the Hindu rosary, from which the Buddhist ones are derived.

The Moslem rosary, called the *tasbih* (which means 'reciter') has 99 beads, plus a special one called the 'leader', or *imam*. The lesser version of the Moslem rosary (which like the lesser Catholic one offers three prayers per bead) has only 33 beads. All Moslem rosaries end with a dangling tassel.

Occasionally there are local customs that forge important links between the rosary and other amulets. A rosary bead may be replaced by a boar's tooth, a lucky stone, or red coral. In this way, prayers are counted with the help of ancient, pagan charms – a deft amalgam of religion and superstition.

Word for Word
INSCRIBED BODY GUARDS

In many countries amulets are worn that include verbal statements, sayings or names.
Strictly speaking, these amulets should be called talismans, although today this
distinction is not always made. The idea behind such Body Guards is that the message
in the writing will be observed and understood by any harmful spirits and will repel
them. Usually the written phrases are religious in nature – words from the Koran or
the Bible, or some other holy book – but there are exceptions to this rule. Sometimes the
words are taken from older, pagan magic, supposedly with ancient mystical powers.
Some verbal amulets proudly display their statements, while others hide them away
in a box or locket. The strength of such devices is that they can be highly specific, but
their weakness is that they only carry any significance for those who speak the
language in question.

ALLAH

It is not easy for Muslims to design an Islamic Body Guard that offers them the visible protection of their deity. This is because it is against their faith to create a pictorial image of Allah or of the Prophet Mohammed. Instead they must limit themselves to the written word. This does not prevent them from wearing sacred amulets of great significance, but it does tend to rob these objects of any immediate visual impact.

THE MOST POPULAR Islamic amulet is a small, flat, rectangular sheet, usually made of gold or silver, on which is inscribed a verse from the Koran. Looking like a tiny page from the sacred book, it displays a special verse in Arabic script. The lettering is too small to read without great difficulty, but this is not a problem for those who wear it because every devout Muslim knows the words by heart. The verse in question is called the *Ayat al-Kursi*, the Throne Verse, and it translates as follows:

In the name of Allah, the Beneficent, the Merciful. Allah! There is no God but He, the Living, the Self-subsisting, the Eternal. No slumber can seize Him, nor sleep. All things in heaven and earth are His. Who could intercede in His presence without His permission? He knows what appears in front of and behind His creatures. Nor can they encompass any knowledge of Him except what he wills. His throne extends over the heavens and the earth, and he feels no fatigue in guarding and preserving them, for He is the Highest and the most exalted. Allah, the Most High, speaks the truth.

The central, written section of the example of the *Ayat* amulet shown here measures only 7 by 9mm (about ⁵⁄₁₆ by ⅜in), which means that the individual words are minute. An alternative way of enlisting the amuletic protection of Allah is drastically to reduce the number of words displayed. This is done on the *Ma Shaa Allah* amulet that is a favourite of parents who wish to protect their babies. Pinned to an infant's clothing, this amulet offers only three words in place of the 104 of the *Ayat al-Kursi*.

The message *Ma Shaa Allah* translates as 'What God has willed!' It expresses wonder at Allah's creation and, although brief, is felt to be suf-

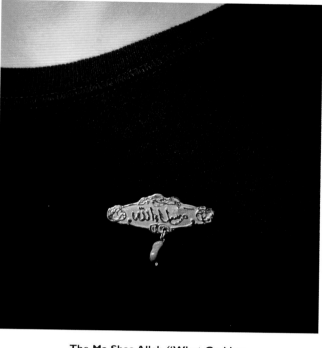

The Ma Shaa Allah ('What God has willed') amulet – a favourite with parents who wish to protect their children.

ficient to provide an adequate defence against any hostile influences that may otherwise harm the precious infant.

An even simpler version is the little blue Allah/Mohammed bead. This modest amulet displays only two words – *Allah* on one side and *Mohammed* on the other – written in Arabic script.

At a distance, none of these three Islamic amulets looks particularly impressive when compared with the images of other major religions. However, the strength of these particular Body Guards is not in their shape or design, but in the massive power that is invested in the words inscribed or painted upon their surfaces.

The small protective bead with the word Allah on one side and Mohammed on the other.

THE GA'U

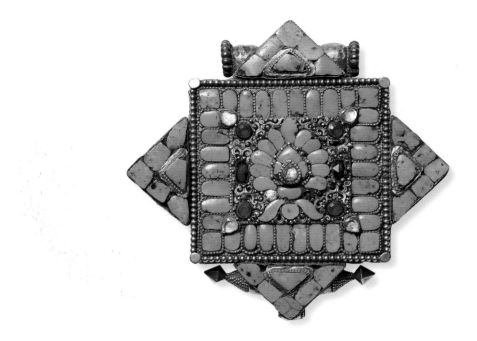

PERHAPS THE MOST beautiful of all protective amulets are the magnificent, jewel-encrusted 'charm-boxes' of the Tibetans. These boxes, known as Ga'u (or Gahu, or Gawo) are worn by high-status Tibetans to protect themselves from misfortune, accident and disease, especially when they undertake journeys. A typical box consists of an elaborate metal container inside which nestles a verbal charm in printed or hand-written Sanskrit. The message is usually a short religious text. Additional or alternative contents include small relics, objects blessed by a lama, fragments of a monk's robe or images of a god or guardian saint.

Sadly, today these dramatic Body Guards are more likely to be found in antique shops or museums than hanging around the necks of their rightful owners. Since the Chinese invasion of their homeland, refugee Tibetans have been forced to sell most of their traditional belongings. An interesting feature of these discarded Ga'us is that, when opened, they are nearly always found to be empty. The Tibetans may have been forced to sell their valuable jewellery but, when doing so, appear to have taken the precaution of removing the most vital parts: the sacred, protective words themselves.

Perhaps these tiny, magical scraps of paper have been carefully encased in simple containers – ones with less commercial value – and even today are playing out their ancient defensive role, carried more modestly on the bodies of their superstitious owners.

A Tibetan woman wearing a traditional costume that includes a large Ga'u.

THE TEFILLIN

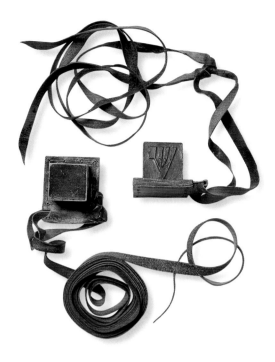

THE TEFILLIN, OR Phylacteries, are two small black boxes containing sacred Hebrew texts that are worn by Orthodox Jews when praying. One box is worn on the arm, so that its texts are directed at the heart and the other is worn on the head, so that the texts are directed at the brain. It is unfortunate that, to the ignorant, the one attached to the forehead looks rather comical, like a little joke hat – a squared-off miniature top hat – when in reality its role is a solemn part of Jewish religious ritual.

The Tefillin are Body Guards similar in function to prayer-wheels, rosaries, amulets quoting the Koran, and the Tibetan Ga'u boxes. They are all objects carried or worn on the body as aids to the holy protection offered by sacred texts or prayers.

Considerable skill and care are involved in the manufacture of the Tefillin. The best boxes are made from kosher cowhide using only the thickest skin, from the cheeks and neck. Only one pair is made from each cow. After cutting, the hide is dried for 3 months, and the whole process of manufacture takes about 11 months. The boxes are sewn together with thread made from veins or tendons. Not surprisingly, a pair of top-quality boxes is one of the most valuable of the religious Body Guards.

The attachment of the Tefillin in preparation for prayer.

The head Tefillin contains four sacred paragraphs from the Torah written on four separate parchments housed in four compartments. The hand Tefillin contains the same four paragraphs on a single parchment in a single chamber. Among other things, the inscribed words offer protection from drought, so that crops and domestic animals will flourish, and food, wine and oil will be plentiful.

151

ABRACADABRA

Amulets bearing the magic word 'abracadabra' have been popular for centuries as charms against ill-health. The explanation given is that the word represents a demon that brings disease. By writing the word in full on the face of the amulet and then copying it again and again, but each time dropping one letter until only the single A is left, the wearer is supposed to see the strength of the demon diminish as his word diminishes.

THE HISTORY OF this strange, magical word has been hotly debated. Some say it is Roman in origin, having been invented by a court physician in his attempts to cure his emperor's fevers. Others think it is much older, believing that it derives from the ancient Babylonian phrase *Abbada Ke Dabra*, which means roughly 'perish like the word' – this clearly being the instruction to the disease-demon.

As often happens with ancient pagan beliefs, major religions co-opt them and adopt them to their own ends. Jewish scholars of the cabbalistic sect suggested that the word 'abracadabra' is derived from the Hebrew words for the

The Abracadabra talisman was popular during the Middle Ages.

holy trinity – the father (*ab*), the son (*ben*) and the holy spirit (*ruach acadach*). With this interpretation they proposed that amulets bearing the magic word would act as powerful charms against evil spirits.

Abracadabra amulets are usually triangular in shape, but there is some disagreement about whether the triangle should be pointing up or down. With the point at the bottom it is suggested that, as the shorter and shorter word is read, starting from the full word at the top, the evil force will progressively lose its strength until it has eventually shrivelled to nothing. With the full word at the bottom of the triangle, the amulet is presumably read from the bottom to the top.

One explanation of the meaning of the magic word Abracadabra sees it as arising from the Hebrew words for the three figures of the Holy Trinity.

Body Parts
ANATOMICAL BODY GUARDS

It is a common practice to employ an image of a particular part of the human body as a protective device. This was especially popular in ancient Egypt, when there were amulets showing the heart, the head, the face, the ear, the eye, the tongue, the fingers, the hand, the arm, the leg and the phallus. Several of these parts of the human anatomy are still widely used on amulets today, in many different cultures. These modern survivors include the heart, the eye, the hand, the leg and the phallus, each with its own specific symbolism. The eye, with its duty to outstare the Evil Eye, and the hand, with its many protective gestures, are both so important that they have been allocated their own separate chapters in this book. The others are grouped together here, along with a few later examples.

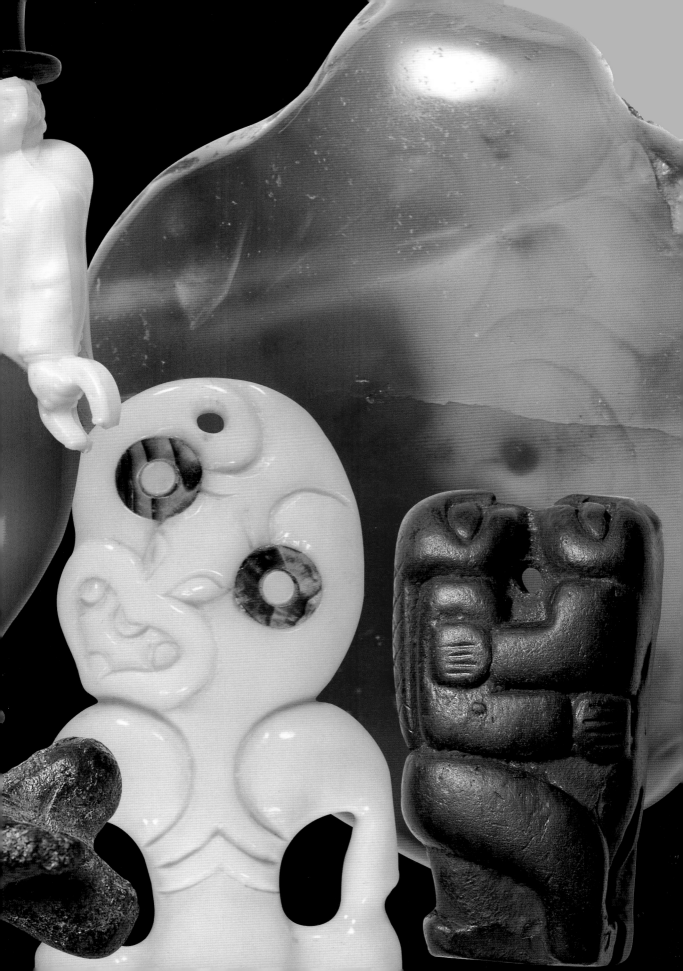

THE HEART

In ancient Egypt the heart was a symbol of life. As an amulet it was designed to prevent the person's heart from making an 'unfavourable utterance'. It was also intended to frustrate the forces of evil that wished to steal the soul from the heart. The Egyptians believed that if the soul left the heart, the body would perish. The heart–soul also became an important image in early Christian art and heart amulets.

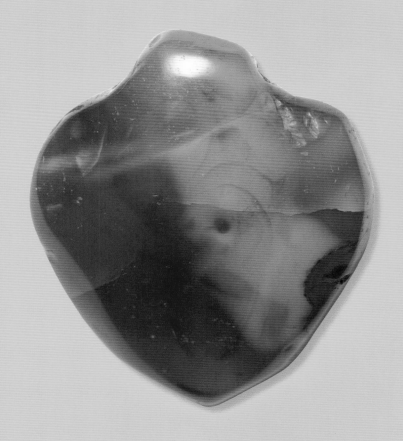

I N THE MIDDLE EAST today, a heart-shaped amulet, inscribed with holy words from the Koran, is still worn as a form of defence against the 'bad eye'.

Over the years heart amulets have been made from almost every imaginable kind of material, from gold to cheap plastic, but in ancient times it was always said that the most effective heart charms were those fashioned from precious or, at the very least, semi-precious red stones. Rubies, bloodstones, red jasper and garnets were the favourite gems, but in early Egypt, cornelian was also popular. A whole section of the Egyptian *Book of the Dead* is entitled 'the chapter of a heart of cornelian'. Less costly heart amulets were made from red glass, red porcelain, red paste or red wax.

A curious feature of the modern heart amulet is its shape. In the oldest examples, hearts were often realistically modelled. The one shown opposite, although crudely carved in cornelian, is much closer to a true heart shape than the well-known later ones, with the familiar 'cleavage' at the top. It has

been suggested that the introduction of this cleavage, which today is obligatory on any heart image, whether three- or two-dimensional, has nothing to do with the heart itself. Certainly it is not visible on the real heart. It appears to be an intrusion of another very basic human body-symbol – the cleft of the female buttocks. It is as if the original heart shape has started to divide into two halves, combining the romantic 'life and soul' element with the sexual 'paired hemispheres' element to create a powerfully evocative double impact. In connection with this, it is noteworthy that, in recent times, the significance of the heart image has slightly shifted, moving from a symbol of life to a symbol of love.

In this new capacity it remains an immensely popular subject for lucky charms and amulets, reflecting the protective, loving attachment of one person for another. If accepted as a lover's gift, the wearing of it becomes a way of guarding the bond between the two people involved. More than any other, this is the amulet that leaps across divides of culture and religion, becoming a truly global protector.

An ancient Egyptian heart depicted on a 1920s cigarette card.

Heart amulets today are made in many materials, in this case snowflake obsidian.

157

THE PHALLUS

One of the most common of all ancient protections against the Evil Eye was the phallus.

It was believed that the exposure of a taboo object, such as an image of the erect male

penis, would divert the forces of darkness and preoccupy them. In that way it would help

the owner of the phallic amulet to escape their destructive attentions. In addition, there is

also an element of counter-threat in the display, which may help to drive away the enemy.

Uninhibited phallic figures were much more common in ancient times.

I<small>N ANCIENT ROME</small>, an amulet depicting the phallus was referred to as a *fascinum*. There were several kinds, some larger to protect houses and gardens, and some smaller to be worn on the body. These phallic amulets took different forms. One of the most popular showed an aroused, curved penis with a glans at one end and a hand making the fig-sign at the other. Hanging from its middle is an unaroused set of male genitals. The popularity of this version was undoubtedly due to its triple message – three male signs for the price of one.

A second form displayed a winged phallus. Another showed one with small bells hanging from it. And yet another portrayed a penis-headed animal with a large erection. These were all widely used in ancient Rome and many have survived to the present day. There are literally hundreds of them in the museums of the world.

In Rome these remarkable amulets were worn openly in the street, and soldiers made great play with them when going into battle. Even small children were adorned with them as protections against the Evil Eye – a malevolent force that was particularly fond of attacking helpless children.

Today phallic amulets are far less common. Even when people are highly superstitious, they no longer feel comfortable about displaying an image of an erect penis in public. In Italy, in modern times, protective amulets are more likely to show the less obviously shocking phallic hand gestures than the phallus itself.

Despite this, the phallic amulet has not vanished altogether. It can still be found in a few regions, especially in the Far East in countries such as Thailand and Japan. Many examples are, however, discreet, in that they display a harmless image which can be opened up to show a hidden phallus within. In this way, the wearer can be protected by a powerful sexual image without causing offence to a friend or a passer-by.

In Thailand, a particularly popular modern phallic amulet is the surprisingly explicit *palad khik*. Its name means 'honourable surrogate penis' and it is believed to have been introduced into Thailand in the eighth century by Cambodian monks. It is worn by men for a double purpose: to protect their genitals from injury and to increase their luck with the opposite sex.

This potent *palad khik* amulet is usually carried on a waist-string that is worn beneath the man's clothing so that it remains hidden from public view. Some men wear several of them in an attempt to give their luck an extra boost. It is hard for the Western mind to grasp that these are not cheap pornographic charms, but serious religious artefacts. The penis amulets bear ancient Buddhist inscriptions in an antique script that can no longer be understood by the modern Thais who wear them, but which still impresses them with its sacred origins. The finest examples are fashioned from horn, bone or wood by monks who specialize in skilled carving.

A phallic amulet from ancient Rome, with a bull's head added for reproductive power.

Palad khik amulets appear in several different designs: sometimes the penis has the hind legs of an animal; sometimes an animal sits on top of it. Animals enlisted in this unusual amuletic duty include the lizard, the crocodile, the monkey, the tiger, the lion and even the snail. The curled tail of the animal often forms the loop for the attachment of the charm.

THE FOETUS

The Hei-Tiki is one of the strangest figurines to be found in the whole of tribal art. It shows a human body with three-fingered hands, tightly bent limbs, huge round eyes, and a large head cocked dramatically to one side. There is nothing else like it, and it has a long and mysterious history.

P OLYNESIAN IN ORIGIN, the Hei-Tiki (which means literally 'tied-on Tiki') is generally recorded as representing the 'ancestor figure' of the New Zealand Maoris. Displayed as a neck amulet and made of polished stone, it was cherished by each Maori family as a treasured heirloom. It was said to be worn by senior members of the family and, upon their death, was passed on to the next in line.

Because the Hei-Tiki was passed from generation to generation in this way, it was often described as the protector of the family name, the family's ancestry and its future. Each Hei-Tiki was given a personal name, was sung to and wept over, and became far more than a mere ornament.

This does not, however, explain the curious posture of the Hei-Tiki figure. This is not a normal, adult human being. As an ancestral or god figure – the 'first Maori' – its anatomy is decidedly odd. It appears to be squeezed up on itself. The explanation is that it is not in fact an adult, nor even a child. It is instead a human foetus, shown in a womb-contained posture. This is why the limbs are so tightly bent back on themselves, why the head is pushed down onto one shoulder, why the head is so large in relation to the body, and why the eyes are so big and round.

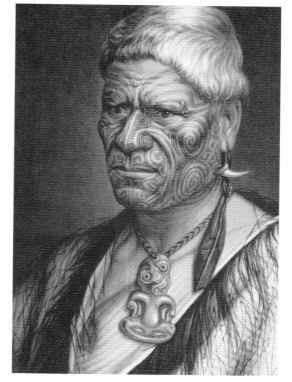

A Hei-Tiki worn by a senior member of a Maori family (from a painting in the Auckland Museum).

A Maori Hei-Tiki depicted on a 1920s cigarette card.

Given this interpretation, the Hei-Tiki's protective role becomes rather more specific. It clearly has to do with fertility and birth. According to one legend, the first Hei-Tiki was made for the goddess of childbirth, Hineteiwaiwa, by her father. After this it was worn by women of high rank as a Body Guard against the envious spirits of stillborn children, which, because they resented the living, were greatly feared by Maoris.

One of the strangest qualities of the traditional Hei-Tiki is the enormous amount of effort that must have gone into fashioning the object. To create each pendant required literally hundreds of hours of hand labour because the nephrite stone employed was unusually hard and extremely difficult to carve. Sizes vary from 5cm (2in) to 23cm (9in) and colours from dark greenish-black to very pale green. Of 85 Hei-Tikis examined, 58 had the head tilted to the right and 24 to the left.

Inevitably, ancient Hei-Tikis are extremely rare today, but they do appear from time to time on the tribal art market, selling at extremely high prices. As a more modest alternative, modern Hei-Tikis that have been carefully carved from greenstone can still be obtained from New Zealand. Inexpensive imitations in green plastic are also commonly available, but whether objects manufactured from plastic will ever be taken seriously enough to be granted special protective powers is highly doubtful.

THE GENITALS

THE MUNACHI, OR Couple Stone, is a popular genital charm from the Andes. Found in both Bolivia and Peru, it has two functions. The first is to attract sexual love and the second is to protect that love once attained. In the language of the Quechua tribespeople, the name Munachi means literally 'to make love happen'.

Although its significance is sexual and it displays genital contact between a man and a woman, the Munachi amulet is discreet in the manner in which it does this. The loving couple embrace one another face-to-face with the woman sitting on the man's lap. The genital contact is implicit but not visible, the active genitals of the pair being completely concealed by their posture.

The Munachi is usually made from soapstone or terracotta and a suspension hole is drilled just beneath the joined, kissing lips. In the West, where it is now widely available as a 'lucky charm', people are most likely to wear it as a pendant on a cord around the neck, but its traditional use is slightly different. Among the Andean Quechua, two hairs are taken, one from each of two lovers, threaded through the hole and tied in a special knot. The amulet is then concealed in a significant hiding place – perhaps under their marriage bed, beneath the floor of their home, or buried just outside it. There it remains forever, a private symbol of their romantic attachment, ensuring (they hope) that their relationship will be a fruitful and lasting one.

THE LEG

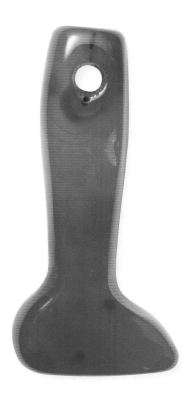

AN AMULET IN the shape of a lower leg and foot was popular in ancient Egypt about 4,000 years ago. Strung together with other elements, it was worn as an anklet and its function was to protect the wearer against the loss of movement or, more drastically, against the loss of a limb. (In Egyptian writing, the leg hieroglyph was used to indicate movement.) The favourite material for this amulet was cornelian, but it sometimes also appeared in ivory, copper or glazed composition.

Being a simple shape, the leg amulet was easy to make and was often added to strings of beads. When these beads were traded abroad, the amulet gradually spread to other countries and eventually managed to reach as far as Scandinavia. There,

where human legs were constantly at risk when travelling across the difficult terrain, it came to be used once more as a protective amulet, guarding against fractures and, where this failed, helping to speed the healing of a broken bone. Early examples, symbolically carved from bone, have been discovered by Scandinavian archaeologists.

As the centuries passed, Scandinavian monasteries started to oppose the use of such pagan symbols and its popularity waned. However, in recent, less intensely religious times, it has returned to favour. It is now once again widely available as a protective body ornament in modern Sweden, where it is no doubt a favourite amulet of local sportsmen and sportswomen, especially skiers.

THE HUMP

In earlier times it was considered lucky to touch the hump of a hunchback. This was especially true in Italy, where amulets of a hunchback figure known as Gobbo, were fashioned in red coral, gold, silver and ivory. They were particularly popular among gamblers, who would hold the Gobbo amulet in their hand and rub its hump as the roulette wheel was spinning, the dice were being thrown or the cards were being dealt.

THE FAME OF THE Gobbo spread around much of the Mediterranean. In the nineteenth century, small silver charms showing a hunchback were popular amulets on sale in the markets of Constantinople. During this same period, they were also the preferred lucky charms in the casinos of Monte Carlo. They even left their mark on the English language. The phrase 'playing a hunch' originally referred to making a play at the gaming tables after touching a hunchback. In France, it was a common practice among Paris stockbrokers to touch the hump of a hunchback before playing the market there.

Even today, in modern Italy, it is possible to buy a cheap plastic key-ring showing Gobbo, the Hunchback, as a protection against the Evil Eye. To make doubly sure of his effectiveness, this Gobbo is depicted holding a horseshoe in one hand and giving the *cornuta* horn-sign with the fingers of his other hand. There is also a large, hollow 'chilli' charm which, if opened up, reveals a tiny Gobbo inside. Curiously, Gobbo was always a male hunchback. Female hunchbacks were said to be as unlucky as the males were lucky.

According to one authority, Gobbo was a descendant of the grotesque ancient-Egyptian dwarf-god Bes. Although extremely ugly, with a deformed, fat, stunted body and a huge, wide, bearded head with a protruding tongue, Bes was one of the most popular amulets employed to ward off evil spirits. His threatening expression, reminiscent of a Maori warrior greeting, and the loud noises he made with the musical instruments he carried, were supposed to frighten off the evil ones. In ancient Egypt his image was everywhere, not only worn on the body but also decorating household goods and buildings. He was employed as a protective amulet by the Egyptians for nearly 2,000 years, from 1500 BC to AD 400, and was adopted by both Greece and Rome. It was probably his transfer from Egypt to ancient Rome that started the tradition which led eventually to the Italian Gobbo.

Eye to Eye
STARING BODY GUARDS

The deep-seated fear of the Evil Eye has meant that wearing a rival eye – a protective symbol that can outstare the evil one – has proved immensely popular over many centuries and in many cultures. 'Eye idols' have been known since prehistoric times, and in ancient Egypt the famous Eye of Horus was one of the most important of all sacred amulets. Since then, staring eyes have been employed on jewellery, on buildings, both inside and out, on great ships and on small fishing boats. Today they are still found in dozens of different cultures scattered all over the world, from Portugal to Turkey and from Malta to Bali.

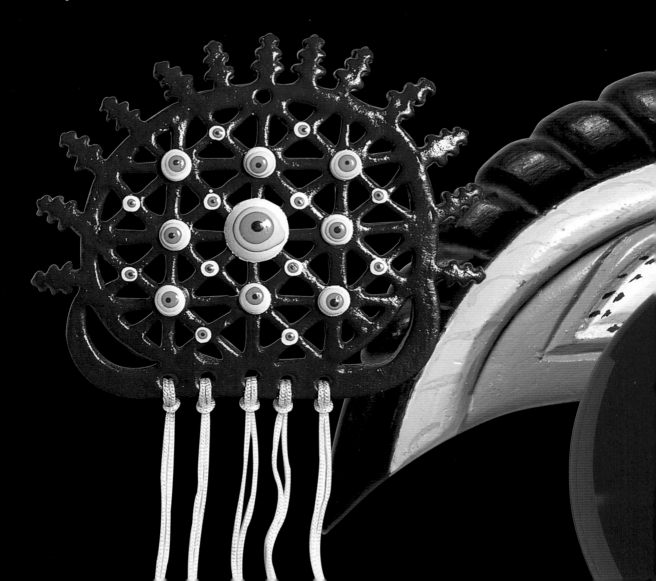

THE EYE OF HORUS

In ancient Egyptian mythology the sun and the moon were the (right and left) eyes of the falcon-god Horus. When he opened them there was light; when he closed them there was darkness. It followed from this that amulets of the Eye of Horus were the most important of all Egyptian Body Guards and had widespread powers.

THIS ALL-SEEING eye, also known as the Udjat or Wedjat Eye, was said to be capable of observing all the evil that existed in the world. From Egypt its influence spread outwards to Greece, Rome and other cultures around the shores of the Mediterranean. Still popular today as an amulet, it is reputed to bring protection against theft, ignorance, poverty and ill-health. And it has often been seen as the ideal protection against the Evil Eye, which it is capable of outstaring.

The Eye of Horus always has the same unusual and highly characteristic structure. There is a strong eyebrow, clearly defined eyelids, a large round pupil, and two strange marks underneath the eye. One of these marks drops straight down from the centre of the lower eyelid. The other is a diagonal stroke that ends in a tight curl. If this were a human eye, one would have to say that the vertical mark is meant to represent a tear-stain and the diagonal one a single, huge eyelash. But a glance at the facial pattern of the African lanner falcon reveals that these two markings are in fact stylized versions of the dark patches that appear on the side of that bird's face, confirming that this is indeed the eye of the great falcon-god.

In ancient Egypt a pair of these eyes was often placed on the door recesses of tombs, on coffins and on sarcophagi. There they stood, staring out forever, protecting the mummified bodies inside against all forms of evil and ensuring that they would be left in peace to make their long journey to the afterlife without hindrance.

A modern keyring bearing the Eye of Horus. The ancient Egyptian amulet on the opposite page is several thousand years older.

BOAT EYES

People are especially vulnerable when travelling and many Body Guards are seen displayed in cars and lorries, on working horses and on boats and ships, protecting the travellers from the countless dangers they face.

A Maltese fishing boat equipped with a pair of ever-staring bow-eyes.

BOATS SAILING THE waters of the Mediterranean Sea have been protected from the Evil Eye for over 2,000 years and there is no sign that this practice is fading today. The risks of drowning or, in the case of fishing boats, of failing to make a good catch ensure that, at sea, ancient superstitions are still alive and active.

The major form of Boat Guard has always been a pair of bow-eyes. Positioned one on either side of the vessel's prow, these eyes provide an ever-present glare, always ready to outstare the Evil Eye, should it approach. Eyes of this kind are known from ancient Egyptian, Greek, Etruscan, Roman and Phoenician ships and can still be seen on boats today, although now only on smaller fishing boats.

The most dramatic eyes in modern times are found on the fishing craft of southern Portugal, Malta and Gozo. The Portuguese eyes are usually painted onto the wood of the boat using dramatic black lines and with a long, curving eyebrow. The Maltese and Gozitan eyes are more three-dimensional, with thick, carved eyebrows and sometimes with glass eyes embedded in the modelled wood. Like the bodies of the boats, these eyes are brightly coloured and their impact leaves no doubt about their magical task of staring down any opponent. They are carefully re-painted each year.

Maltese boat-eyes are usually hand-carved from wood and then painted in bright colours.

EYE-AGATE

E YE-AGATE (also sometimes called Eye-stone or Aleppo Stone) has been used as a protection against the Evil Eye since ancient times. When it was realized that layered agate could be cut in such a way that it created a circular eye pattern, it became a popular stone for making amuletic beads and rings. The idea that an 'eye' could exist in a natural stone probably helped to make it seem unusually magical. Early examples of eye-agates are known from both ancient Egypt and the Orient.

A special kind of eye-agate is found in the Sudan, where there are black agate stones with circular white markings. These are ideal for making vivid, staring-eye amulets, which are said to be

Inexpensive, modern eye-beads worn today as lucky charms.

especially efficient at outstaring the dreaded Evil Eye.

Because eye-agate was so expensive in earlier days it was not long before inventive craftsmen found a cheaper substitute in the form of glass eye-beads. These appear to have been invented independently by the ancient Egyptians and the ancient Chinese over 2,000 years ago. They later became popular all over the world and are still manufactured in large numbers today.

THE BLUE EYE

I N TURKEY the most common form of protective object is a Blue Eye. Known locally as Nazur Boncuk, or Evil Eye Stone, it may be worn as a decoration, carried as a key-ring, hung in a car or a bus, or placed in a house.

There are hundreds of design variations, from a single, simple blue eye to a complex, ornate multi-eye. But they all have two things in common: the presence of at least one eye and the presence of the colour blue. The possession of one of these objects is thought to protect the owner both from attacks by the Evil Eye and from misfortune in general.

Some Turkish Blue Eye amulets are combined with other protective symbols, promising a double protection. There are, for instance, horseshoes with multi-blue-eyes, and Hands of Fatima with a Blue Eye in the centre of the palm. These variations appear to be recent and are probably aimed more at the tourist trade than the local inhabitants, who seem to prefer to hang up a single, large, dramatically simple Blue Eye made of shiny glass.

The fame of the Blue Eye has spread far and wide. This example is from Egypt.

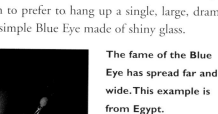

Helping Hands
GESTURAL BODY GUARDS

Hand gestures have been used as protective actions in many parts of the world and these actions have often been 'frozen' as hand amulets. They have the advantage that, while they are being worn, they never stop making the protective sign. A protective hand gesture is a fleeting action, over in a second, but an amulet carved in the shape of that gesturing hand can be worn for years. The stronghold for this particular kind of Body Guard today is Italy, although gesturing amulets are also popular in Spain and Portugal and their ex-colonies in South America. Most of the gestures are hostile and protect the wearer by threatening and driving away hostile forces. A few are friendly and protect the wearer by offering the hand of peace to possible enemies.

THE FIG-SIGN

The fig-sign is made by closing the hand in such a way that the tip of the thumb protrudes from between the first and second fingers. It is another ancient gesture with a long and confusing history and it is seen, not only as a fleeting hand gesture, but also in the form of carved amulets dating back to antiquity and still in use today.

THIS IS CLEARLY an obscene signal. It is often stated that the thrusting of the thumb between the bent fingers provides a sexual symbolism in which the thumb becomes the penis inserted into the vagina, with the bent fingers as the female labia. According to one view, however, the thumb is only secondary in this symbolism and is there merely to indicate the presence of the female genitals. If this is true, then to display the fig gesture is to make some comment about female sexuality, without reference to the male element.

In some countries, especially Portugal and Brazil, the fig-sign transmits a protective message, based on the idea of diverting the Evil Eye. When threatened by some supernatural force, the gesturer makes the sign of female genitals with his hand, and this so preoccupies the evil spirit that it is distracted from its malevolent purpose and the gesturer escapes unharmed. Hans Licht, in his study *Sexual Life in Ancient Greece*, makes the following comment:

The exposure by a woman of her organ of generation – with which action the gesture of the 'fico' (fig) is associated – broke magic spells, and consequently its image or symbol was carried as an amulet. The exposure of the organs was especially efficacious against hail, bad weather, and storms at sea…Instead of representing the actual female organ on amulets it was suggested by symbolism, and usually in the guise of the fico (fig)…These amulets were made of very different sizes and of every kind of material – they were carried singly or in batches strung together…They could be carried openly or secretly, and so convinced were people of their power that their mere possession was considered sufficiently effective.

In many countries today these amulets have outlived their magical, sexual origins and are sold simply as 'lucky charms'. They can be seen in their hundreds in curio shops all over the world and are even on sale in cities such as London, where the fig gesture itself is virtually unknown. It is doubtful whether many of the people who buy these little ivory, stone or wooden hands have the slightest notion that they are purchasing, and then boldly wearing, a symbolic set of female genitals.

The question remains as to why the gesture should be called a 'fig'-sign. The answer is that, presumably because of its appearance, the fig has since ancient times been seen as a symbol of female genitals.

In some traditions, the Tree of Knowledge in the Garden of Eden is seen not as an apple-tree but as a fig-tree. When Eve presented Adam with the fruit of the tree, she was not giving him an innocent apple, but offering him her fig – her sexual organ. And later she covered it with a fig-leaf – not a leaf *from* a fig-tree, but one that *covered* her fig.

Reinterpreting the Garden of Eden story in this way makes a great deal of sense, and it is not difficult to see why, in ancient rituals, the idol of Bacchus was always made from the wood of the fig-tree, and the most sacred object in the Bacchanalian procession was a basket of figs.

THE V-SIGN

The V-sign is given by thrusting the hand up into the air, with the first and second fingers extended and separated from one another to create a V-shape. The other two fingers are held back by the thumb. The palm of the hand faces inwards towards the body of the gesturer.

THE V-SIGN IS A confusing gesture, having two completely different meanings, depending on where you live. If you are from the British Isles it carries a hostile message. If you are from any other part of the world it is a friendly, celebratory signal indicating 'Victory'.

The hostile meaning

In Britain and Ireland the V-sign is the most savage insult known. To wear it as a protective amulet would be to offer a permanent, powerful threat to any adversary. In fact, it is so virulent that as an amulet it is comparatively rare, although some examples do exist.

Its origin is controversial, and many explanations have been given. The current favourite sees it as having its beginnings in the 15th century, at the battle of Agincourt. The story goes that the French had issued a warning before the battle, saying that when they won they would cut off the 'bow fingers' (the first and second fingers of the right hand) of the English archers, making it impossible for them ever to fire arrows again. When the battle ended with an English victory, the English archers taunted the French prisoners by holding up their bow fingers to remind them of their failure to carry out their threat.

A detailed geographical survey in the late 1970s revealed that it was understood by everyone in England, Wales, Scotland, Northern Ireland and Eire, but by nobody at all in continental Europe. Outside the British Isles it was only known in regions that had experienced a strong British presence during colonial days.

There is, however, a weakness in this theory. If it began simply as a military taunt, why is it widely considered to be so obscene? When large numbers of British males were asked to give an explanation of why the gesture is so rude, not one of them knew of the Agincourt theory, but they did offer a variety of sexual explanations for what the V-sign represents. These included: an enlarged phallus, a double penis, inserted fingers, female genitals, and widely spread female legs.

The friendly meaning

Outside the British Isles the V-sign nearly always means 'Victory'. This is a comparatively modern gesture that has spread rapidly around the world. It was invented on 14 January 1941 by a Belgian lawyer called Victor de Lavelaye. He was looking for a symbol for the wartime resistance movement – something which could be used as graffiti to annoy the Nazis. The word for 'Victory' started with the same letter in most languages so seemed suitable. His idea was taken up by the BBC, who added the Morse code signal for V (dot-dot-dot-dash) and a musical counterpart in the form of the first four bars of Beethoven's Fifth Symphony. Winston Churchill then extended this idea even further by converting the V-sign into a hand gesture, only with the palm facing out, rather than backwards as in the insulting gesture. The V-for-Victory campaign swept through Europe and successfully enraged the Nazis, who failed to stamp it out.

Some V-sign amulets signal a V-for-victory over the forces of evil.

Other V-sign amulets oppose the forces of evil with an obscene threat.

THE ALOHA

Sometimes a friendly greeting gesture finds itself elevated to the level of a Body Guard and people start to wear it as a protective amulet. The gesture says 'be happy' and, by wearing it in the form of an amulet, its owner is, in effect, displaying his or her non-aggressive mood, thereby reducing the chance of unpleasant encounters.

A STRIKING EXAMPLE OF a friendly gesture that has developed along these lines is to be found today on the Hawaiian Islands. There, a special local greeting involves holding the right hand aloft with the thumb and the little finger erect. The other three fingers are bent forward. With the hand in this position, the Hawaiian wags it gently in the air. It is the gestural equivalent of 'Aloha!' All over the islands it is possible to buy small images of hands performing this gesture, to be carried as amulets or used as stickers on cars or other vehicles.

Few inhabitants of the islands understand the origin of this gesture. To them it is 'just traditional' – the usual reply when origins have been forgotten.

A study of its history reveals that it is a modified Spanish gesture. At some point in the history of the Hawaiian Islands, Spanish sailors, or immigrants from the Spanish cultures of Central or South America, must have brought it with them. On arrival they no doubt wished to show they were friendly by inviting the locals to join them for a drink. In early days Spaniards drank out of small leather bottles which they held up to their mouths so that a jet of liquid was poured straight into their open lips. Tourists in Spain today are sometimes encouraged to drink the local wine in this ancient manner, possibly because the novelty of the action makes them forget the quality of the drink they are being offered. And even today, the Spanish (and South American) gesture for 'come and have a drink' is a mime of the action of tilting up a leather bottle. The Spanish gesture consists of erecting the thumb and little finger and then pointing the thumb towards the open lips. This must have been the action that those early Spanish-speaking visitors made towards the local

The Aloha gesture worn as a 'good luck' lapel badge in modern Hawaii.

Hawaiians when they arrived upon their shores. The Hawaiians learned its friendly meaning and began to imitate it. But because it now stood for 'friendly greeting' rather than 'come and have a drink', they omitted the directional element of the gesture. Instead of pointing the thumb towards the lips, they simply held the hand aloft and waggled it back and forth, combining the Spanish drinking gesture with a cheerful wave. As time passed, the old form of the gesture was gradually forgotten, until it became known simply as the local greeting. And today nobody realizes that when they make this gesture they are using a Spanish drinking signal hundreds of years old.

It is now popularly known as the 'Aloha' or 'Hang Loose' gesture. Some inhabitants of the islands today also call it the 'Shaka' gesture, because of its repeated use by a local television comedian called Lucky Luck whose catch-phrase was 'it's a shaka' (ie 'it's a shocker').

The Aloha gesture is also seen as a 'good luck' car-sticker in Hawaii.

THE FOREFINGER

IN RECENT TIMES, born-again Christians of North America have taken to making a special sign, with one forefinger raised stiffly aloft, and with the other digits bent. This sign is meant to indicate that there is only one true God – namely theirs. The gesture carries a vigorous message of religious affirmation and an unspoken threat to all non-Christians, suggesting that their idea of God is not the true God.

Amulets of this gesture have recently appeared, although they do not seem to have become especially popular. Not only do such amulets have to compete with the all-pervasive Christian image of the cross, and to some extent now the fish, but also there is a rival gesture in the world of sport and entertainment. There, winners will often make the upright forefinger sign as a way of celebrating their victory by saying 'I am No. 1'.

The forefinger gesture, with added Christian cross, worn as a 'One Way!' lapel badge.

THE HIDDEN THUMB

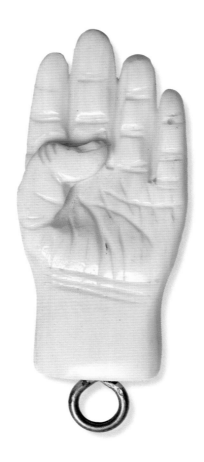

IN ANCIENT ROME, when gladiators fought in the Colosseum, the crowd would signal its approval or disapproval, at the end of a contest, with a hand gesture. If the beaten man had fought badly they would mime the act of stabbing him. This was the 'thumbs down' gesture. If he had fought well and they wished him to be spared, they covered up their thumbs in a gesture called the *pollice compresso* – the 'compressed

The 'hidden thumb' gesture worn as a 'good luck' neck pendant.

thumb'. By mistranslation this 'thumbs covered up' gesture became altered to 'thumbs up', which has survived into modern times as a well-known indication of satisfaction or approval. But the true gesture, with the thumb hidden, has managed to survive in some places and can still be found in the form of a small, protective amulet made of metal or bone. By wearing this sign of generous approval that originally spared a life, the owners of the amulet presumably hope that their gesture of generosity to others will bring similar rewards to them.

CROSSED FINGERS

'Keeping your fingers crossed' is one of the most common of all protective gestures in the Western world. Because of its popularity, a representation of a hand with crossed fingers is sometimes worn as a protective emblem or amulet.

WHEN MAKING this gesture, the middle finger is twisted over and around the forefinger, while the other two fingers are bent back fully and held under the thumb. The hand may be raised slightly as the fingers are crossed, so that the 'locked' forefinger and middle finger point upwards, or the hand may be held forwards, with the crossed fingers in a horizontal position. The posture is usually held for only a few seconds. A common variant occurs with the hand held behind the back or in some other hidden position, so that although visible to a companion, it is concealed from a third party.

The most popular explanation of this gesture is that it is a religious sign that has broken loose from its devout origins to become a 'common superstition'. This interpretation suggests that the act of crossing the fingers was originally a cryptic version of making the sign of the Christian cross. Instead of crossing himself or herself openly in the usual way, a Christian could ward off evil or hostile influences by making a 'cross' with the fingers, an action small enough to be easily concealed from unwelcome eyes. Such protection is called upon if the person making the gesture is facing some kind of risk, and feels the need of God's aid, or if he or she is behaving badly in some way – telling a lie, for instance – and wants protection from retribution.

There are, however, three other suggestions. The first sees it as a special form of the *mano pantea*, the ancient hand posture used as a Christian blessing. In this, the hand is held up with the thumb, the forefinger and the middle finger erect, and the other two fingers bent. The three erect digits represent the Holy Trinity, with the thumb standing for God, the forefinger for the Holy Ghost, and the middle finger for Christ. By placing the middle finger over the top of the forefinger, a gesture is formed which is said to represent 'Christ Victorious'. This can be seen in El Greco's *Christ* in Toledo Cathedral, in the 16th-century mosaic of *Christ Pantocrator* in St Mark's, Venice, and in still earlier mosaics at Ravenna. A second alternative ignores Christian influences. According to this suggestion, to cross one's fingers when wishing someone luck goes far back to a belief that magic can tie things together. Here the two fingers are seen, not so much struggling to form a convincing cross, as straining to tie themselves into a knot.

Yet another interpretation that has been offered sees the crossed fingers as the childlike act of crossing something out, a familiar enough action in the world of clumsy childhood writing. It is argued that to keep the fingers crossed while lying is a child's trick and that it 'crosses out' the wickedness of lying or protects the soul against the Devil's seizing it at the moment of sin.

The most likely interpretation remains the first one, that to cross the fingers protectively is to make a stylized form of the Christian sign of the cross. As might be expected, the use of crossed fingers as a protective device is almost unknown in non-Christian countries. It is also slightly less common in Catholic countries. There, the full crossing of the body is more likely to be made when protection is needed. Because they still use this larger gesture, devout Catholics have little need of the 'meaner' gesture of crossing the fingers. So, for them, a crossed fingers amulet would have no appeal. If they were to seek the protection of the Christian cross in amulet form, it would be as a crucifix worn around the neck.

THE HORNED HAND

In Italy there is a well-known hand gesture called the mano cornuta *– the Horned Hand – that is used as a protection against the Evil Eye, or against anyone thought to be sinister or threatening. The gesture carries such a powerful message that it has graduated from a fleeting action to the level of a small amulet that can be worn on the body as a permanent defence against evil.*

The Horned Hand amulet worn today as a lucky charm, often by people who have no idea of its long history.

WHEN MAKING THE gesture, the hand is pointed forward, with the forefinger and the little finger extended horizontally. The other two fingers are held down in a bent position by the thumb, giving the hand the crude shape of an animal's horned head, lowered as if to charge. Sometimes the hand is held still and sometimes it is jabbed forward in the air. If the gesturer wants to hide his action from the person at which it is aimed, he may keep his hand down by his side, or even in his pocket.

This gesture originated long ago, in pre-Roman times, and is more than 2,500 years old. It is known from wall-paintings in ancient Etruscan tombs, and from early pottery of the Daunian culture which flourished in east-central Italy around the middle of the first millennium BC.

In its earliest role, the gesture was essentially a device for self-protection. By making the sign of the horns, the gesturer was supposed to be able to defend himself against evil spirits, the Evil Eye or any other form of misfortune that might seem to be threatening him. In this capacity, the horns were being used in their primary symbolic role as representing the defensive power of a great horned animal, almost certainly the bull. The use of the gesture in this way reflects an even older practice, that of placing a pair of horns on the wall of a building, to protect it and its occupants from evil forces.

From the early bull divinity, there developed a horned god which, with the rise of Christianity, eventually became converted into the horned devil-figure. Today, people often refer to the horn gesture as 'making the sign of the Devil's horns', and when they use it protectively they are, in effect, reinstating the Devil in his earlier beneficial role as a defending deity.

The use of the gesture is concealed whenever the gesturer suspects an evil influence but for reasons of etiquette does not wish to bring the matter out into the open. If such caution is abandoned, then the hand is whipped up into a directed pointing posture, aiming straight at the face of the person thought to possess the Evil Eye. Alternatively, if the evil force is considered to be a generalized, diffuse emanation of some kind, then the gesture may be made by waving the hand around in all directions.

The wearing of amulets depicting the Horned Hand has been commonplace for at least 2,000 years, and examples are still sold today in everything from gold to plastic. They can be found in curio shops all over Europe – from London in the north, to the Canary Islands in the south. They are referred to simply as 'lucky charms' and it is doubtful whether, in many cases, either the sellers or the buyers are aware of their long and ancient history.

Modern versions of the horn-sign can be purchased today in some car-accessory shops in Mediterranean countries. These consist of self-adhesive plastic horn-signs that can be fixed to the rear of a car or a truck to protect its occupants from the vehicle following behind them. Other examples can be found on small boats.

THE MIDDLE FINGER

A WIDESPREAD GESTURE of hostility that is now sometimes displayed as a Body Guard is the middle-finger gesture. This gesture involves an upward-thrusting movement of a stiffly erect middle finger, with the other fingers and the thumb held fully bent. The finger symbolizes the erect penis and the other digits represent the testicles on either side of it. As a powerfully explicit phallic gesture it is reserved for moments of intense anger or scorn.

This is one of the oldest of all obscene hand gestures and was particularly popular in ancient Rome, where it was known as the *digitus impudicus* – the 'indecent finger'. The outrageous Emperor Caligula enjoyed the scandal of offering his extended middle finger when inviting one of his subjects to kiss his hand.

Although the middle-finger sign is understood in many different parts of the world, its modern stronghold is North America, where it is known simply as 'The finger'.

The wearing of an amulet of the middle finger gesture implies that its owner is indicating his defiance of the world, protecting himself by offering a hostile threat to anyone who might wish him harm.

The ancient Roman phallic gesture popular today in America as a savage insult, and sometimes boldly worn in the form of an amulet.

188

THE MOUTZA

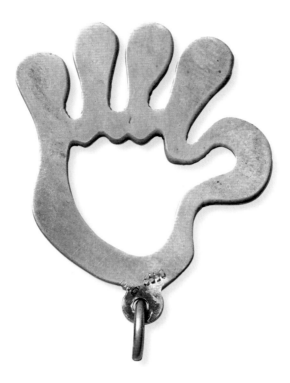

IN GREECE TODAY it is possible to buy a small ornament that can be worn on a chain around the neck, showing a hand with all the fingers and the thumb spread out as widely as possible. To non-Greeks this looks innocent enough – like an open hand being pushed towards you – but to Greeks it is a savage insult, known as the *Moutza*.

In origin the Moutza is an ancient Byzantine gesture. It dates from the time when criminals were chained up and put on display in the streets, where they could be tormented and abused by the local population. A favourite way of doing this was to scoop up a handful of filth and thrust it into the helpless captives' faces. The forward thrusting of an open hand came to symbolize that action. Performing this movement carried the message 'I would like to push filth in your face'.

The vicious Moutza sign has proved to be amazingly tenacious. Even though the modern hand that makes the gesture is both empty and clean, and regardless of the fact that most modern Greeks have no idea about its ancient origins, the 'palm-thrust' action remains, to this day, the worst of all Greek insults. It is not only performed as a gesture (especially in tense traffic situations) and worn on the body as a protective amulet, it is also available as a brightly coloured car-sticker.

One of the problems of local rude signs of this kind is that foreigners rarely understand them. To a non-Greek the gesture appears to be saying no more than 'keep back', as the palm is thrust towards them. Indeed, visitors to Greece can easily make the mistake of using this action themselves to ask someone politely to move back, with unexpected results.

THE HAND OF FATIMA

One of the most popular Body Guards in the Middle East today is an artefact that consists of a downward-pointing hand. The fingers are close together and the hand is flat. Small examples are worn on the body as protective amulets and larger ones are hung up in the house.

THIS OBJECT IS generally known as the Hand of Fatima, but among Arabs it is also called the Hamsa Hand. *Hamsa* means 'five' and simply refers to the number of digits on the hand. It is also found in India where Hindus call it the Humsa Hand. Jews refer to it as the Hamesh Hand or the Hand of Miriam. The legend of its origin is as follows:

A Jewish version of the Hand of Fatima, called the Hamesh Hand, from the city of Jerusalem.

The daughter of the Prophet Mohammed, the Lady Fatima, was busy preparing food when her husband, the prophet Ali, arrived unexpectedly. To her dismay Fatima saw that he was accompanied by a beautiful young concubine. The sight of Ali with his new companion tormented her but she remained silent and continued to go about her work in the kitchen. In her confusion she did not notice what she was doing. She had been preparing halva in a hot pan, and when she saw Ali with his new love, she dipped her hand down into the hot halva and began stirring it. She was so distraught that she did not feel any pain, but her husband was horrified by what he saw and rushed over to her, shouting a warning. Only then did she realize that her hand was burning and took it from the hot pan.

As a result of this incident, the downward-pointing Hand of Fatima became an important symbol throughout the Middle East. It has been displayed for centuries in the form of a necklace of small hands, as a single amulet on a chain, or as a wall-hanging. It is believed to bring good fortune to its owners and to endow them with the virtues of patience and faithfulness.

There are a number of variations in the design of the Hand of Fatima. The fingers are shown in two different ways. In the more realistic form there is a thumb and four fingers, while in the more stylized version there are three central fingers with a short thumb on either side making the amulet appear more symmetrical.

In some hands there is an eye in the middle of the palm, offering the additional protection of the 'eye that outstares the Evil Eye'. This is sometimes called the Eye of Maat. Some of the larger, ceramic hands also display sacred writings to boost their power. And there are sometimes extensions of the fingers in the form of blue beads, or little bells.

With the Hindu version, called the Humsa Hand, the central eye seems to have become more important than the hand that surrounds it. In Asia, where the amulet is considered to be a particularly powerful Body Guard, it is often referred to by the alternative name of the All-seeing Eye of Mercy.

The Jewish version – the Hamesh Hand – may be shown inverted, that is to say, pointing upwards, and when it is in this position it may have four small fishes hanging from its 'wrist'. Other types, showing the hand in the correct, downward position, may instead have the four fishes portrayed on the surface of the four fingers.

This protective hand has now spread to the New World, and the Jewish version sold today in California has proved to be wonderfully adaptable. Instead of defending people against feelings of anger in the face of unfaithfulness (a lost cause in California, cynics would say), it has been cunningly adapted to protect its owners from the dangers of major earthquakes.

A small Turkish Hand of Fatima, worn as a pendant, and combined with a protective Blue Eye.

THE RING-SIGN

The ring-sign, in which the thumb and forefinger make a circle, is an example of a common gesture with more than one meaning. In much of the world it indicates that everything is fine. In some regions, however, especially the Middle East, the ring shape symbolizes an orifice, and the action of making the sign is seen as a gross obscenity.

So it is important to know the source of a ring-sign amulet before trying to interpret it.

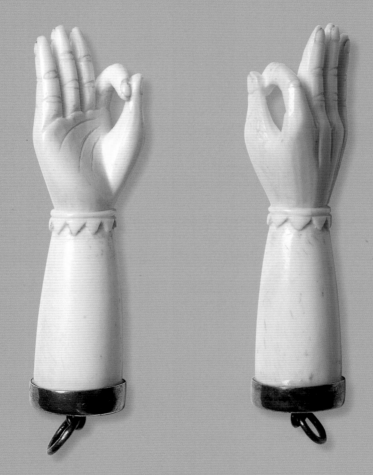

IT SEEMS LIKELY that the 'everything is fine' message of the ring-sign is a 20th-century export from America that has spread rapidly across much of Europe, replacing the much older, obscene message in many regions. This has happened, for example, in Spain, where today most people interpret the gesture in the new way. But this was not always so. In the British Museum there is a lovingly fashioned Spanish protective amulet in the form of an obscene hand making the ring-sign. The hand is made of carved ivory with two gold rings on the fingers, one with a garnet and the other an emerald. The gold sleeve is skilfully decorated with red, blue and green enamel and it ends in an elaborate silver ruff.

This amulet was worn in Spain in the 16th century and is officially listed as 'a higa, a fist-shaped amulet directed against the evil eye, with the characteristic position of the thumb and forefinger…a potent gesture directed against evil'. According to the British Museum: 'A similar hand-shaped pendant of wood and enamelled silver has been considered an ex-voto of Charles V of Spain.'

Frederick Elworthy, who, in his classic (1895) work on the Evil Eye, devotes a whole chapter to protective hand amulets, singles out the ring-sign for special mention:

…the hand in this position is…commonly made and sold as an amulet against the evil eye, although the gesture itself is not one…As a gesture, however, it may be one of the most insulting…there is a distinct flavour of defiance, and perhaps on that account it may have been adopted as an amulet in the concrete form… This gesture is called the Phallic Hand.

Elworthy probably uses the term 'phallic' because the hand forms a genital-like orifice.

To understand the meaning of this wooden ring-sign amulet it is necessary to know its country of origin.

He illustrates two hand amulets displaying the ring-sign, one small one made of coral, for personal wear, and a larger metal one used as a 'horse amulet'. The latter was found on a horse-drawn cab, employed to protect either the animal, the cabman, his passenger, or all three.

In a search for modern examples of this amulet, a well-made one was found in the Canary Islands. The seller could not, or would not, explain its symbolism, stating only that it was to be worn to 'bring good luck'. If, as seems likely, this is yet another case of an obscene hand gesture being employed as a protective device, it once again was working on the principle of distracting the Evil Eye, preoccupying it and therefore deflecting the danger. It is a simple piece of logic to suppose that, if the Evil Eye is very wicked, it will be fascinated by the most obscene images one can offer it.

The sexual ring-sign employed to protect a horse-drawn cab on the streets of 19th-century Naples.

Safe as Houses
HOUSE GUARDS

The homes where we live are so important to us that we take special steps to guard them and to protect ourselves when we are in them. In addition to modern burglar alarms, security systems and guard dogs, we also occasionally employ more ancient methods. Magical, protective objects are placed in the garden, hung near the front door, displayed inside the hall or fixed to a wall. Most of these have a long and complicated history but have managed to survive into modern times because of the powerful, natural fear that so many people have about the safety of what is, for the owners of the property, the most important place on earth. It could be argued that these House Guards are not true Body Guards, but this is misleading because the primary purpose of this type of object is to protect the occupants of the house, rather than the building itself.

THE DREAMCATCHER

If a spider's web can act as a trap for unpleasant insects, it is only a small leap of the imagination to seeing it as a trap for unpleasant experiences. For some Native North Americans, this led to the creation of the Dreamcatcher. This is an artificial web that can be hung near the bed of a child, or even an adult, to trap bad dreams and prevent them from entering the sleeper's head at night.

According to Native North American legend: 'In the night air there are good dreams and bad dreams. The good dreams go through the web and into the one sleeping, while the bad dreams become hopelessly tangled in the web, where they perish at the first light of dawn.'

The earliest Dreamcatchers were hung over cradles to protect children from nightmares. Today adults also use them and they are especially favoured by romantic lovers, who hope that they will encourage blissfully fulfilling dreams about the ones they adore.

In recent times these Dreamcatchers have become available commercially. The one shown here consists of an abstract, circular web with a small black bead representing the spider. Hanging from the outer ring of the web are seven long feathers, connected by blue beads. These feathers are said to assist the flight of the good dreams.

With the recent resurgence of interest in Native North American mythology, Dreamcatchers have become so popular that there are several sources for them and a variety of styles. The traditions are slightly different from tribe to tribe.

All Dreamcatchers have a circular hoop, attached to which are a web and hanging attachments, but the details vary. The hoop was originally made of willow and covered with sage. Today it is made of either wood or metal and in both cases is covered with leather. The web itself was made of deer sinew, but this is now forbidden and modern Dreamcatchers have webs made of artificial sinew. Sometimes the web is decorated with many beads, sometimes with just one and sometimes with none at all. Some webs have a large hole in the centre, through which the good dreams pass. Others lack this hole and the good dreams must find their way through any available gap. The number of feathers

Some Dreamcatchers are small enough to be worn around the neck, as protective pendants.

hanging from the circle also varies: usually there are between three and seven, although there may be only one.

It is generally accepted that the Dreamcatcher tradition first started with the Ojibwa Indians and then spread out among other Algonquian tribes, including the Cree. Most tribes seem to agree that it is the good dreams that pass through the web and the bad dreams that get caught up in it, but there is an exception to this rule. According to the Lakota, the opposite is true, as can be seen from the following abbreviated version of the Lakota legend.

Iktomi, the great trickster and teacher of wisdom, appeared in the form of a spider and spoke to an old Lakota spiritual leader. According to the legend, 'As he spoke, Iktomi the spider picked up the elder's willow hoop which had feathers, horse-hair, beads and offerings on it, and began to spin a web.' When he had finished spinning, he gave the elder the web and said:

The web is a perfect circle with a hole in the centre.
Use the web to help your people reach their goals,
making good use of their ideas, dreams and visions.
If you believe in the great spirit, the web will catch your
good ideas and the bad ones will go through the hole.

To anyone who has purchased a modern Dreamcatcher and hung it over their bed, this is confusing, but they should take heart in the thought that, whether their nightmares are trapped *in* the web and disposed of in the morning light, or whether they escape *through* the web and are banished for ever, the basic message is the same: with a Dreamcatcher you should be able to enjoy a peaceful night full of sweet dreams.

THE SWASTIKA

Seldom can a protective sign have been so badly tarnished as the ancient swastika. For centuries, this wheel of life acted as a beloved guardian of all who wore it. Then, in the space of a few, horrific years, it became the most hated symbol in the world, having been adopted by Adolf Hitler and his Nazi followers. It will doubtless take many centuries for the swastika to regain its original role as a revered Body Guard, if it ever does.

As a protective symbol, the swastika has been active in many cultures – Asia (Hindu, Jain, Brahman and Buddhist); the Orient (China and Japan); the Americas (Mayan and Navajo); Europe (Etruscan, Roman, Germanic, Celtic); Scandinavia (including Iceland); the Mediterranean (Libya, Sicily, Malta, Crete, Mycenae, Cyprus, Rhodes, Greece); and the Middle East (Persia and Mesopotamia).

In some distant regions, remote from World War II, the swastika is still employed in its old, protective role. In rural Tibet, for example, farmers sometimes place a swastika above the door of their dwellings to prevent the entry of evil spirits. On the other side of the world, Navajo medicine-men fashion protective swastikas on the ground with coloured sand as part of their rituals.

The name 'swastika' originates from the Sanskrit word *svastika*, meaning well-being or good fortune. Its precise symbolism has been hotly debated. Particular meanings given to it include sacred fire, living flame, productive power, the daily rotation of the sun, the sun-wheel, revival and prosperity, fecundity, lightning, the storm, Thor's hammer, the wind, the four levels of existence, the movement of the seasons.

There is general agreement, however, that the 'crooked cross', as Winston Churchill called it, represents a 'spinning cross'. As the simple, central cross rotates, its movement is indicated by the right-angled pieces at the ends of the arms, as if they are streaming light or fire. Despite all the variations, the central theme does seem to be the sun and its movement through the sky. Since the arrival of the sun brings heat, light and energy, the swastika inevitably symbolizes the daily rebirth of life. Just as the sun protected people from cold and darkness, so its emblem, the swastika, protected them from harm. In this way it became the good-luck symbol of many very different cultures.

There has been some confusion about which way the swastika should point in order to bring good luck. To calculate the direction of the rotation of a swastika, envisage each of its four arms as an arrowhead pointing in the direction of rotation. In ancient times it had to be rotating clockwise and this was the version first recommended to Hitler by Friedrich Krohn, the man responsible for introducing the emblem to the Nazi movement. For some reason Hitler insisted on reversing it so that it was indicating movement in an anti-clockwise direction. To many ancient cultures this would have symbolized not good fortune, but bad fortune, but perhaps Hitler's thinking was to thrust this bad fortune under his opponents' noses. Or perhaps he merely wished to distance himself from any early, sacred values. A new pagan cult arose within the Nazi movement and its hymn began: 'The time of the Cross has gone now, The Sun-wheel shall arise…'

For Hitler, the swastika symbolized a special kind of rebirth – the revival of national life. It became the emblem of the national flag of Germany from 1935 to 1945. Once it had become closely identified with Nazism, its new association quickly obliterated all its earlier meanings. One of the world's greatest protective symbols had become the most despised.

THE CORN DOLLY

Making Corn Dollies – small images fashioned from twisted, dried straw – is a popular folk-art that has survived for centuries in Europe. At most country fairs it is still possible to find a stall selling a variety of these figures, created in a number of traditional designs. Some are shaped to look like small female figures, others like bells, lanterns or hearts. The oldest patterns (like the one on this page) are called 'fans' and are more abstract.

T AKEN HOME AND hung up in the house, these pagan artefacts are seen today as little more than innocent, rural decorations. The truth, however, is that they are far less innocent than they seem. If their real significance was understood, they might be viewed in a rather different light and be displayed less readily.

Originally, the Corn Dolly or Corn Doll (the word 'doll' is short for 'idol') was part of a fertility ritual. During the annual harvest, as the crops were being cut down, the corn-spirit had to flee into what was left of the uncut corn. Eventually she was trapped in the very last sheaf of standing corn. If this was thoughtlessly scythed down, it would mean that the protective corn-goddess would be destroyed and no crops would grow the following year. To protect themselves against this disaster, early farmers fashioned a small 'Mother Goddess' figure from the straw of this last sheaf, carried her into their house and kept her safe there until the following spring.

While she resided in their house the Mother Goddess (also known as the Harvest Queen, the Old Woman, the Maiden, the Hag or the Harvest Dame) protected the farmers from a barren future. In the spring, she was taken back into the fields again and her spirit was allowed to enter the newly sown seed of the next year's crops. In this way the new seed would be awoken and another good harvest was ensured.

As agriculture became increasingly mechanized, and farmers less and less superstitious, the corn-goddess began to fade from view. Corn Dollies were almost lost from folk culture. But in a few remote areas they managed to survive, and gradually, in the 20th century, they have been revived as a minor, decorative art form. Their pagan significance is largely ignored and they have become more and more 'polite' and culturally 'correct', their original, arcane symbolism long since forgotten.

The old, pagan fertility goddess, who protected the farmers' crops, still lives on today in the form of the Mother Earth Corn Dolly.

This process has been aided by the addition of a number of modern motifs that have little to do with the ancient beliefs. In addition to the traditional forms, there are now Christian Crosses, Hearts, Crowns, Shepherd's Crooks and even Umbrella Dollies. But the earlier motifs have also persisted and exist today with names such as the Herefordshire Fan, the Bearded Fan, the Welsh Border Dolly, the Neck Dolly and the Mother Earth. It is clear from the design of many of these more ancient forms that the symbolism involved is intensely sexual. Because the corn-goddess was concerned with the fertility of the crops and because she became symbolically embodied in female form, it was inevitable that the next step was to focus on her organs of reproduction. The traditional 'fan' pattern is, in reality, an imaginative exaggeration of the human female genitals. They have become sufficiently 'abstracted' to make them inoffensive to innocent eyes, but their long history of pagan fertility worship leaves no doubt about their true nature. Hanging in the kitchens and halls of pre-industrial farmhouses, they were the perfect protectors of the fertile earth so crucial to the survival of the early farmers.

Today the pleasures of purely decorative Corn Dolly plaiting are on the increase in Europe. In North America the custom has also been spreading since the late 1970s. There it is known as Wheat Weaving and there is even a 'Wheat Weaving Resource Center' and a National Association of Wheat Weavers. Significantly, with this new, sanitized form of the pagan folk art, the patterns and motifs are referred to simply as: 'Abstract shapes or religious symbols...to insure prosperity and good luck in the next growing season.'

SHEELA-NA-GIG

It comes as a shock to devout Christians to discover that many of their early churches were adorned with outlandishly obscene stone carvings. These were generally placed on an outside wall of the building and consisted of a naked female figure displaying her greatly enlarged genitals. To make matters even more explicit, she is often depicted in the act of holding her genitals open with both hands.

WHY ON EARTH would the original Christian designers of early churches instruct stone-masons to carve such grotesque, sexually explicit decorations? The answer usually given is by now a familiar one. Because they are so evil, the Devil and his kin are particularly fascinated by sexual motifs. Obscenity acts as a powerful distraction, claiming the full attention of the forces of darkness and diverting them from other mischief. The presence of these lewd figures on the outsides of churches was believed to preoccupy the evil ones so greatly that they would forget about their wicked desires to enter the sacred buildings and cause havoc there. In this way the Christian souls praying inside the churches would be kept safe from devilish interference.

These extraordinary female figures go by the mysterious name of Sheela-na-gigs. There are dozens of them, scattered widely across England, Wales and Ireland. Similar figures are found on churches in France and Spain. Although their general role did become protective, their origins were more complex. They were probably first commissioned as grotesque warnings about hell. The females portrayed are not appealing, but repellently ugly. They were whores condemned to burn in hell and were originally placed on the buildings to create a stark contrast between those in the pews, who were pious and saved, and those up on the walls, who were lascivious and lost. The message of the medieval churches was clear – pray now for redemption, or you too will end up like *that*. To put it another way: prayer is beautiful – lust is ugly. But people everywhere are superstitious, never more so than in medieval times, and it is clear that the Sheela-na-gigs soon became widely viewed as yet another weapon against the intrusions of the Evil Eye. What began as a morality lesson ended up as a scare-Devil.

Perhaps the most astonishing feature of the extraordinary Sheela-na-gigs is that they managed to survive the prudery of the Victorian period. Some were defaced on the orders of sensitive vicars and others were removed from the outer walls and hidden away. But many were left in place and a recent detailed survey of the churches of western Europe has produced detailed maps showing that there are still, to this day: 25 in England and Wales; 54 in Ireland; 20 in Spain; and 49 in France.

A Sheela-na-gig (on the right) displaying herself on the church wall at Kilpeck in Herefordshire.

On the opposite page: A small Sheela-na-gig in the form of a modern pendant amulet.

MISTLETOE

THE FAMILIAR CHRISTMAS tradition of kissing under the mistletoe tends to conceal the fact that this strange, parasitic plant has a deeper symbolic significance as a protector of houses and stables. For centuries it has been considered as a defence against devils, witches and demons when put up over a building or hung inside it. Because the entrance hall of a house is the place where the plant was most conspicuously displayed – to stop the evil spirits entering when the front door was opened – and because this was also the part of the house where greeting kisses were exchanged as visitors arrived, a link was forged between the mistletoe and the kissing. In addition, the close proximity of the mistletoe helped to protect the kissing couple themselves in their happy moment.

Why should mistletoe, a poisonous parasitic plant that is seeded by sticky bird-droppings clinging to the branches of trees, have such a powerful symbolic role? There have been three suggestions:

♣ The oak and the mistletoe are seen as male and female. This endowed the mistletoe with a sexuality that transformed it into a fertility symbol.
♣ The mistletoe was thought to grow where the great oak had been struck by lightning, making it a symbol of protection against fire.
♣ The cross on which Christ was crucified came from a tree that was so ashamed of itself that it shrank to a small parasitic plant which must live out its life attached to other trees. The mistletoe therefore becomes a symbol of the Holy Cross.

THE RED RIBBON

IN SOUTH AMERICA a common ailment, known as *mal de ojo*, or 'Evil Eye', is observed in babies and infants. The symptoms are vomiting, diarrhoea, colic and dehydration. Parents believe that it is caused, not by lack of hygiene, food poisoning or some kind of virus infection, for which they themselves might be responsible, but by the mystical damage caused by the baby being stared at by someone possessing the Evil Eye. It is thought that body energy of the staring adult is transmitted to the child and that, since this energy is unsuitable for the sensitive child, it sets up internal body disturbances. So, instead of improving hygiene or diet, the parents rush to their offspring's aid by tying red ribbons to the cot, around the bed, or on the baby carriage. This colourful display is intended to hold the attention of the adult, drawing his or her gaze from the baby itself and in this way shielding the child from harm.

In Jewish communities this practice is also commonplace. Here it is often felt necessary to add more and more red ribbons as the days pass. Every time a visitor comes to the house to see the new arrival, peers at the baby and praises its good looks (as visitors nearly always do) the parents must add one more red ribbon, or *royte baendel*. Each of these ribbons is called a *kayn aynhorah*, which translates as 'may no evil harm you'.

In some countries these protective ribbons may also be attached to the baby itself, being tied around its wrists and ankles, used as hair-ribbons or fixed to the clothing.

THE HORSESHOE

In the Western world it has long been a tradition to nail an old horseshoe above the door of a house, barn, stable or church, to protect the building and its occupants from evil forces. As an extension of this custom, small replicas of horseshoes have often been made and sold in the form of portable amulets, to be worn on the body as lucky charms.

ALTHOUGH THE LUCKY horseshoe's main duty is as a House Guard, it also plays a symbolic role in several other contexts. In some countries, a bride is provided with horseshoe-shaped ornaments at her wedding, to bring her good fortune. And, in earlier days, many a lucky horseshoe went to sea, firmly nailed to the ship's mast. Even Admiral Nelson succumbed to this particular superstition and had one fixed to the mast of the *Victory*.

In more recent times, the horseshoe has resurfaced in a modified form that goes unnoticed by the casual observer. Superstitious taxi-drivers who seek its protection will go to great lengths to ensure that the number-plates of their cabs contain a letter U. In this way they can display a permanent, symbolic horseshoe-shape, even if they are forbidden to decorate their vehicles with the real thing.

It is sometimes said that if the horseshoe is nailed on a building with its open end pointing downwards (in an inverted U), all the good luck will run out and be lost. For successful protection, it is claimed, the horseshoe must be nailed in place with its two points uppermost. The U-shape will then act like a container, holding the luck in place.

A rival opinion, which sees the horseshoe shape as a pair of devil's horns, demands that the horseshoe should be placed in the inverted-U position, so that 'the Devil will run out of it'. A third view is that the horseshoe should be on its side, with the points facing to the right. In this way it makes a letter C, standing for Christ, and therefore providing Christian protection for the building.

It is also solemnly pointed out that if the horseshoe is not securely fixed in place it will bring you bad luck – because when you open the door it will fall on your head and you will end up in hospital.

There are various explanations as to why a simple, practical object like a horseshoe should possess magical powers:

♣ The horseshoe is made of iron. Iron is commonplace today, but in ancient times it was so precious that it was endowed with supernatural powers. In some cultures, iron objects were placed on the corpse to protect it from the attentions of evil spirits. In others, people 'touch iron' for good luck instead of touching wood. A Hindu bride wears a protective iron bracelet at her wedding. One theory suggests that, since meteorites were an important early source of iron, superstitious people may have looked upon the metal as a gift from the gods, giving it an almost sacred quality.

♣ The horseshoe is a sexual symbol. Others believe that the horseshoe has a powerful symbolic impact because its shape is reminiscent of female genitals. This may sound far-fetched, but in some ancient images the female sex organs are stylized in such a way that they do look remarkably like horseshoes in shape. And the placing of a sexual symbol above a door, as a way of catching the Devil's attention, distracting him, and preoccupying him long enough to deflect him from entering the building, is well known (see page 202–3).

♣ The horseshoe is a symbol of the new moon. Some see a link between the curved shape of the horseshoe and the new moon. The crescent shape of the new moon is frequently employed as a protective device and, with a little imagination, the tips of the horseshoe become the points of the new moon.

♣ The horseshoe is a symbol of a pair of horns. Others see the upright U-shape as a metal equivalent of a pair of animal horns. Horns are often used to protect buildings in the Mediterranean region and a discarded horseshoe could easily have been a simple way of acquiring a 'horned defender', when true horns were in short supply.

♣ The horseshoe protects the horse without causing it pain. Before the anatomy of the horse's foot was understood, it was thought to be strange and magical that a piece of metal, taken red-hot from the blacksmith's fire and fitted on the animal's hoof, did not hurt. If it could burn the hoof without causing pain it must surely have amazing protective qualities.

Because of the horseshoe's protective power, even the nails that hold it in place are said to have magical properties. Rings fashioned from these nails give their owner the same kind of protection as the horseshoe itself. Adding to their mystical power is the fact that there are always seven of them on each shoe, seven being the most important of all 'lucky numbers'.

It has even been suggested that, in architecture, the design of the archway, with its semicircular top, originally had the same significance as the inverted-U shape of the horseshoe, and that the original function of the archway, when it replaced simple, rectangular doorways, was to act as a built-in protective device for churches and other important buildings.

The most extraordinary horseshoe display in the world is to be found at Oakham Castle in Rutland, England. There, the high walls of the 12th-century Great Hall are completely covered in a collection of over 200 horseshoes. The Norman baron who lived there insisted that every nobleman who visited the castle should leave behind one horseshoe, which would be fixed to the castle gates. The practice is still continued to this day, but for safety the horseshoes have been moved indoors.

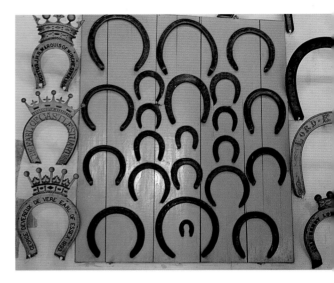

The amazing Great Hall of horseshoes at Oakham Castle.

The earliest Oakham Castle horseshoes are unmarked, so that it is impossible to decide exactly when this custom began, but we know for certain that the practice dates back more than 500 years. The oldest identifiable horseshoe on show, presented by King Edward IV, is dated 1470, and the most recent one, presented by the Lord Chief Justice of England, is dated 1981.

Some of these shoes are enormous. The 1470 one is 100cm (39in) wide, about seven times the size of a practical horseshoe. Clearly the King wanted to impress the locals with his gift and had the shoe specially fashioned for the castle gates. Many of the later ones are elaborately decorated with crests and emblems. Queen Elizabeth II, who left a shoe there in 1967, did not follow this competitive 'show-off' trend. Instead she honoured the Norman baron's original request of supplying a shoe from the visitor's own horse. Her horseshoe was from one of her royal racehorses.

If a horseshoe does indeed bring good luck to the building displaying it, the Great Hall of Oakham Castle must be, without question, the most fortunate building in the world.

If one horseshoe brings a little luck to a building
and its occupants, then it follows that many horseshoes
should bring an abundance of good fortune.

EKEKO

T HE MOST POPULAR HOUSE GUARD in the region of the South American Andes is Ekeko, the Aymara god of fortune or god of abundance. By placing his effigy in your house it is believed that you will be protected from misfortune and all your wishes will come true.

Originally Ekeko was a native hunchback figure, carved out of stone. In modern times the stone has been replaced by brightly painted ceramic, and over the centuries, colonial influences from Spain have seen him transformed into a white-skinned, open-mouthed, mustachioed figure carrying all your wishes on his shoulders.

Ekeko is celebrated at an annual festival on 24 January, when new images of him are bought from

To keep Ekeko happy, he must be given cigarettes to smoke. The longer the ash, the better the luck he brings.

shamans in the Indian markets to bring good luck for the year ahead. Special wishes for the year are also bought, in the form of miniature representations of, say, a bag of food, a television set or a banknote, and these are hung on his body. Before he is taken home, he is blessed by the shaman, who passes him through sacred smoke.

Ekeko, suitably draped with the special wishes, is now placed in the house of his new owner, who does his best to please the god by offering him alcohol, coco leaves and a cigarette. The reason that Ekeko figures always have an open mouth is that the cigarette is lit and then placed between his lips. If he then continues to 'smoke' the cigarette down its whole length, this will increase the chances of the annual wishes coming true.

Today roughly 2 million people still speak the 4,000-year-old Aymara language. They are centred in Bolivia, but are also found in Peru and Chile.

THE SPIRIT BALL

Throughout Europe in earlier centuries (and in some countries even to this day) it became important to have some kind of protection from the Evil Eye. One way to provide this protection was to outstare the Eye. This could be done with an image of a staring eye, but a better solution was to provide a small mirror in which the hostile Eye would see its own reflection and in this way would be defeated by its own evil rebounding onto itself. Unfortunately a single mirror only pointed in one direction, so all that the Evil Eye had to do was to enter the building from some other direction and the mirror would be useless. The answer to this problem was an object called a witch's ball – a coloured glass sphere that reflected the eye from any and every direction.

Like mistletoe, these heavy, early glass baubles were originally hung up in the entrance hall of a

house to stop the evil one slipping through the front door when it was opened to guests. But then a way was found to make them much lighter, so that they could be hung on Christmas trees, and that is where we usually see them today. Most people, however, see them merely as attractive decorations and have no idea about their magical origins as protective devices.

Recently it has become possible to obtain larger versions of these baubles, for use out of doors, to protect the garden. Known as Venetian Globes, these 15cm (6in) glass balls, usually blue, green or silver in colour, are displayed in flower-beds by fixing them onto wooden stakes. They are particularly popular in Italy, where they have been employed since the 17th century to bring 'happiness, peace and prosperity'.

A large blue Spirit Ball, known as a Venetian Globe, protecting a flower garden.

THE ENDLESS KNOT

ENTER A HOUSE in the high Himalayas and you may see hanging on the wall, above either the door or a window, a strange, convoluted shape. This is the Endless Knot, one of the Eight Lucky Things (sometimes called the Eight Glorious Symbols) of Buddhism. It is usually in the form of a piece of carved wood and acts as a defence against ill-health and early death.

The pattern of the Endless Knot is a continuum that represents eternity and immortality. Hanging the amulet near a door or window is intended to prevent evil spirits from entering the dwelling, causing sickness or death to the occupants. In many ways it is the Buddhist counterpart of the lucky horseshoe, except that it is hung on an inside wall instead of outside an entrance.

Also known as the Knot of Eternity, and believed to have originated in China, this design was used as a mandala for contemplation. Its twists and turns, and its nine inner spaces and eight outer spaces, played an important role in the meditative process. To some devout Buddhists, the pattern was a representation of the Buddha's entrails, elegantly arranged as he sat in solemn meditation.

The example shown here came from a house in northern Nepal. Curiously, similar never-ending knot motifs are common in early Celtic designs. But bearing in mind the huge distance between the Celtic world and that of the Buddhists, this can be little more than a coincidence, with two cultures independently adopting the concept of an eternal 'line without end'.

THE HAGODAY

THE HAGODAY IS a door-knocker of a building offering sanctuary. It consists of a head of a monstrous beast holding a heavy ring in its mouth.

Fixed to the main entrance doors of ancient holy buildings, Hagodays played a special protective role. When a hunted person was seeking the safety of sanctuary, it was said that if they could reach the door, grasp the handle of the Hagoday, knock on the door and remain clinging to the metal ring, they were fully protected and their pursuers would be powerless to seize them. Hagodays survive on the doors of many cathedrals, but it is doubtful if today they receive many calls for their assistance.

Traditionally, a Hagoday must have the head of a beast beneath which there is a large handle.

A CHARMED LIFE

IN THIS JOURNEY through the colourful and sometimes fantastic world of amulets and charms, it has become clear that there are several basic principles at work. These can be summarized as the Six Laws of Body Guards.

1 The First Law of Body Guards states that if you are threatened by evil spirits, you can defeat them by *calling on your religious beliefs to come to your aid.* Like fights like. Supernatural threats can be dealt with by supernatural means. Victory is assured because the religious powers that are mustered in defence are those of powerfully organized religious institutions against which a puny little Devil, or a demon or two, stand little chance. Show them a cross or a Buddha and they are soon on the run.

2 The Second Law of Body Guards states that if you are threatened by evil spirits, you can defeat them by *standing up to them and threatening them back.* For those who prefer to fight their own fights, there is a choice of a variety of rude gestures and obscene insults, from the fig-sign to the ring-sign and from the finger to the V-sign.

3 The Third Law of Body Guards states that, if you are threatened by evil spirits, you can defeat them by *diverting their attention.* Because the evil spirits are, by their very nature, wickedly lascivious, they cannot resist a sexual display. By showing them

The protective crucifix obeys the First Law of Body Guards.

a crudely genital image, such as the explicitly sexual carvings on many ancient Christian churches, it is possible to distract them and preoccupy them long enough to break their spell.

4 The Fourth Law of Body Guards states that if you are threatened by evil spirits, you can defeat them by *outstaring them.*
From the sacred Eye of Horus in Egypt to the heavenly Blue Eye of Turkey, and from the ever-open eyes of the Mediterranean fishing boats to the reflected eyes in the highly polished horse-brasses of Europe, people have found ways of fixing a baleful, unblinking stare on the Evil Eye that forces it to look away. As soon as it has done this it has admitted defeat and the day is won.

5 The Fifth Law of Body Guards states that if you are threatened by evil spirits, you can defeat them by *bombarding their senses.*
When a hostile force is envisaged as taking the form of the Evil Eye (as so often is the case), then it should be possible to drive it away simply by dazzling it with bright lights. This is the concept that sees the owners of working horses spending hours polishing their horse-brasses until they glisten in the sunshine. As the smooth metallic surfaces flash, the Evil Eye is forced to look away and, once again, the battle is over. Alternative methods are to scare off the hostile force with an irritating noise or bad smell. Tiny, jingling bells on working horses or a strong whiff of garlic in the home are reputed to work wonders.

6 The Sixth Law of Body Guards states that if you are threatened by evil spirits, you can defeat them by *summoning up the forces of nature.*

Whether animal, mineral or vegetable, the natural features of the planet are always available to assist in the war against the demons of darkness. Carefully selected, protective beasts, magic minerals and warrior weeds are there to serve the beleaguered minds of the victims of superstition.

Amulets in a scientific age

Today we have abandoned many of the early amulets. Instead we protect ourselves with pills and potions from the pharmacist and the doctor. We subscribe to pension funds, take out expensive insurance policies and install elaborate security systems in our houses. If we are rich enough, we may even employ the ultimate protection of professional, human Body Guards.

We keep the evil spirits at bay by jogging, visiting therapists, eating health foods and avoiding the pleasures of the flesh that might attract the attention of the powers of darkness. Some of these activities are truly protective but others are, in reality, simply the latest in a long line of superstitious practices. Only today they wear better disguises.

There is no evidence that those who regularly attend the gymnasium, to experience the masochistic thrill of the 'burn', live longer than those who simply enjoy a relaxed walk. Earnest joggers, if they manage to run long enough and hard enough, are liable to inflict more damage on their bodies than if they had taken a leisurely stroll. Those who pour their hearts out to therapists, to exorcize their demons, rapidly lose the stabilizing independence of private self-examination. Those who follow modern diet fads and forget that they belong to an omnivorous species that thrives on great food

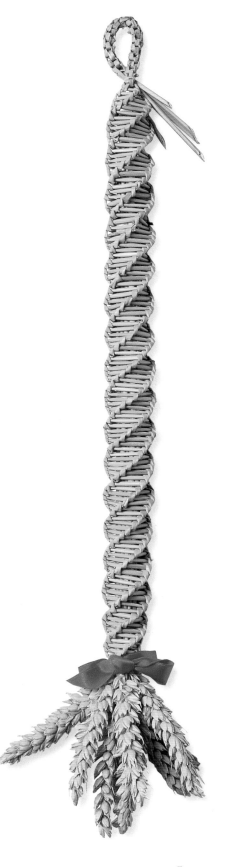

A traditional Twist Dolly to protect the farmer from a bad crop the following year.

variety, are so concerned about their health that the very stress of worrying about it destroys them long before anything else has the chance.

Although it is easy today, in a scientific era, to laugh at the early beliefs concerning the power of a bizarre array of amuletic protections, it is worth remembering that, if the ancients really believed in them, those amulets will have done more good than many of our modern methods. The key point about all such 'protectors' is that, if accepted, they gave peace of mind in a fear-ridden world. That peace of mind will have provided a massive boost to the immune systems of the wearers of those 'magic' amulets, and that boost will have helped to protect them from all kinds of illnesses and ailments. Our modern methods of keeping healthy often do just the opposite – they obsess us with stresses and anxieties that are our greatest enemies.

If someone once believed that to carry a particular kind of crystal would protect them from cancer, it would actually do so. This would not be because of some mystical psychic energies or magnetic fields emanating from the stone, but because

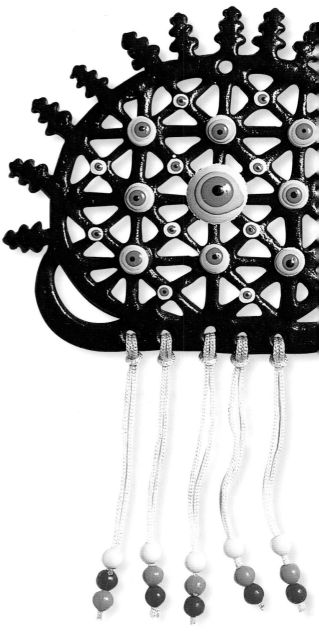

The single forefinger, pointing to the skies to ask for heavenly protection.

A Turkish multi-eye. If one Blue Eye protects you well, then many eyes must guard you even better.

the human brain that accepted the protective value of the stone would rest easier in that thought. And by resting easier, the body of the crystal-wearer would relax a little. Its stress levels would decrease slightly and, in doing so, would increase the efficiency of the immune system. In this way, what to us may only be a silly little crystal would genuinely help to protect against cancer.

Today, by contrast, we know all too well and all too rationally that science, after sacrificing countless millions of laboratory animals, has so far failed to find a cure for cancer. If we are well informed on the subject, as most of us are today, this knowledge makes us anxious. And our anxieties depress our immune systems and we therefore become more susceptible to cancer.

The problem of living in a scientific age is that, although we have made huge advances in technology and enjoy immense benefits as a result, we have also in the process lost the old comforts of believing in magical protection. It is up to science now to provide us with its own, genuine solutions that will replace our old, occult beliefs. If scientific thought convinces us that to wear a particular crystal will not prevent cancer, then it is up to science to replace our belief with something new. If it fails then all it will have done is to rob us of an old superstition but put nothing in its place.

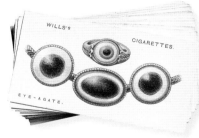

Dreamcatchers have become more popular in recent years.

The famous four-leaf clover worn as a lucky finger-ring.

An epidural anaesthetic is certainly better than a jade amulet at relieving the pain of a difficult delivery, and the drug Viagra is more effective than the wearing of any phallic amulet. But there are many other medical problems that have yet to find their epidural or their Viagra. Eventually we will get there, and all our problems will be solved by scientific discovery, but in the meantime it is little wonder that so many people in so many parts of the world secretly, and sometimes openly, still call upon the aid of one of the hundreds of ancient Body Guards. They rely upon these amulets and talismans to see them through another day full of fears and threats, some real, some imaginary, as they do their best to keep misfortune at arm's length for as long as possible…

These protective *enati*, or Eye-Stones, were made by carving layers of agate in a special way.

Despite its small size, this tiny ram amulet remains a powerful fertility charm.

BIBLIOGRAPHY

Andrews, Carol, *Amulets of Ancient Egypt* (British Museum Press, 1994)

Armstrong, Edward A, *The Folklore of Birds* (Collins, 1958)

Bayley, Harold, *The Lost Language of Symbolism* (Williams & Norgate, 1912)

Binder, Pearl, *Magic Symbols of the World* (Hamlyn, 1972)

Brelsford, Vernon, *Superstitious Survivals* (Centaur Press, 1958)

Bruce-Mitford, Miranda, *The Illustrated Book of Signs and Symbols* (Dorling Kindersley, 1997)

Budge, E A Wallis, *Amulets and Superstitions* (Oxford University Press, 1930)

Cirlot, J E, *A Dictionary of Symbols* (Routledge & Kegan Paul, 1962)

Clair, Colin, *Of Herbs and Spices* (Abelard-Schuman, 1961)

Clough, T H McK, *The Horseshoes of Oakham Castle* (Rutland County Museum, 1987)

Collett, Peter, *Foreign Bodies* (Simon & Schuster, 1993)

Cunningham, Scott, *Encyclopedia of Magical Herbs* (Llewellyn Publications, 1997)

David, Judithann H and Van Hulle, J P, *Michael's Gemstone Dictionary* (Affinity Press, 1990)
Eichler, Lillian, *The Customs of Mankind* (Heinemann, 1924)

Elspeth, Marguerite, *Crystal Medicine* (Llewellyn Publications, 1997)

Elworthy, Frederick Thomas, *The Evil Eye. An Account of the Ancient and Widespread Superstition* (John Murray, 1895)

Elworthy, Frederick Thomas, *Horns of Honour* (John Murray, 1900)

Fontana, David, *The Secret Language of Symbolism* (Pavilion Books, 1993)

Gonzales-Wippler, Migene, *Complete Book of Amulets and Talismans* (Llewellyn Publications, 1991)

Hammerton, J A (Editor), *Manners and Customs of Mankind* (Amalgamated Press, 1931)

Hill, Douglas, *Magic and Superstition* (Paul Hamlyn, 1968)

Holbeche, Soozi, *The Power of Gems and Crystals* (Piatkus, 1989)

Hole, Christina, *English Traditional Customs* (Batsford, 1975)

Howes, Michael, *Amulets* (Robert Hale, 1975)

Johari, Harish, *The Healing Power of Gemstones* (Destiny Books, 1988)

Jones, Alison, *Dictionary of World Folklore* (Larousse, 1995)

King, C W, *The Natural History of Gems or Decorative Stones* (Bell, 1867)

Knowlson, Sharper T, *The Origins of Popular Superstitions and Customs* (Werner Laurie, 1934)

Lambeth, M, *Discovering Corn Dollies* (Shire Publishing, 1994)

Leach, Maria (Ed.), *Folklore, Mythology and Legend* (New English Library, 1972)

Lorie, Peter, *Superstitions* (Simon & Schuster, 1992)

Maloney, Clarence (Ed.), *The Evil Eye* (Columbia University Press, 1983)

Maple, Eric, *Superstition and the Superstitious* (Barnes, 1972)

Meerloo, Joost A M, *Intuition and the Evil Eye* (Servire, 1971)

Meller, Walter Clifford, *Old Times. Relics, Talismans, Forgotten Customs and Beliefs of the Past* (Werner Laurie, 1930)

Melody, *Love is in the Earth. A Kaleidoscope of Crystals* (Earth-Love Publishing, 1995)

Morris, Desmond, *Bodytalk. A World Guide to Gestures* (Jonathan Cape, 1994)

Morris, Desmond *et al.*, *Gestures. Their Origins and Distribution* (Jonathan Cape, 1979)

Murdoch, Tessa, *Treasures and Trinkets* (Museum of London, 1991)

Oakley, Kenneth P, 'Animal Fossils as Charms', in: Porter, J R & Russell, W M S (Eds), *Animals in Folklore* (Brewer, 1978)

Oakley, Kenneth P, 'Decorative and Symbolic Uses of Vertebrate Fossils', in: *Occasional Papers on Technology*, No. 12, 1975, Pitt Rivers Museum, Oxford

Pavitt, William Thomas and Pavitt, Kate, *The Book of Talismans, Amulets and Zodiacal Gems* (William Rider, 1914)

Potter, Carole, *Touch Wood: An Encyclopaedia of Superstition* (Michael O'Mara, 1988)

Roeder, Dorothy, *Crystal Co-creators* (Light Technology Publishing, 1994)

Sheridan, Ronald & Ross, Anne, *Grotesques and Gargoyles* (David & Charles, 1975)

Simpson, Liz, *The Book of Crystal Healing* (Gaia Books, 1997)

Tait, Hugh, *Jewellery Through 7000 Years* (British Museum, 1976)

Villiers, Elizabeth, *The Book of Charms* (Lorrimer, 1973)

Vince, John, *Discovering Horse Brasses* (Shire Publishing, 1994)

Walker, Barbara G, *Symbols and Sacred Objects* (Harper, 1988)

Weir, Anthony and Jerman, James, *Images of Lust* (Batsford, 1986)

Zammit-Maempel, George, 'Fossil Sharks' Teeth. A Medieval Safeguard Against Poisoning', in: *Melita Historica*, VI, 4, 1975, pp 391–406

Zolar, *Encyclopedia of Signs, Omens & Superstitions* (Souvenir Press, 1998)

INDEX

INDEX

ACKNOWLEDGEMENTS

I would like to say a special thank you to the following for their help in preparing this book: David Alexander, Silke Bruenink, Peter Collett, Caroline Earle, Vanessa Fletcher, Estelle Garland, Terry Jeavons, Annie Morris, Jason Morris, Ramona Morris, Shirley Patton, Bill Russell, Guy Ryecart, Miranda Spicer, Michael Whitehead and Alison Wormleighton.

PICTURE CREDITS

Archiv für Kunst und Geschichte, London: 9t (Prado, Madrid), 43t (Louvre, Paris), 97, 113, 119b, 125, 159t, 214
AKG, London/Eric Lessing: 85, 145, 165
Bridgeman Art Library, London: 11b (British Museum), 14 (Egyptian Museum, Cairo), 49b (Bonham's), 64 (Christie's), 73 (San Francesco Upper Church, Assisi), 78 (Museo Archeologico Nazionale, Naples), 79 (Galleria Degli Uffizi, Florence), 134 (British Museum), 137b (Bonham's), 153b (University of Liverpool Art Gallery)
Dr Clive Bromhall: 98
Fortean Picture Library: 47b
Hutchison Picture Library: 81b (Gail Goodyear)
Images Colour Library: 5, 6b, 7b, 159b, 160, 161
Andrew Lawson: 185
Desmond Morris: 10b, 19t, 25, 31t, 32, 35, 37, 39t, 48b, 81t, 85t, 99, 101, 168, 171t, 171b, 198, 208, 210b, 211t, 211b, 213b
Tony Stone: 19b, 26b, 89, 103, 107, 188, 199, 203, 209
TRIP/Art Directors: 33 (C. Rennie), 141 (H.Rogers), 151 (A. Tjagny Rjadno)

Special thanks go to
Clare Bayes, James Cox, Rukshana Chenoy, Maggie DeFreitas, Angela Enahoro, Helene Enahoro, Trevor Gunn, Lucianne Lassalle, M. Parkin and Emma Scott
for help with photography

With thanks to The Healthy House,
A. R. Wibley & Son (Jewellers), Jeremy Hoye (Jeweller)
for the kind loan of props